GOD'S LITTLE DEVOTIONAL BOOK

FOR DADS

RACINE, WI

God's Little Devotional Book for Dads
ISBN: 979-8-88898-033-0 - *Paperback*
ISBN: 979-8-88898-034-7 - *Hardcover*
ISBN: 979-8-88898-035-4 - *Ebook*
Copyright © 2023 by Honor Books, Racine, WI

Cover Design by Faille Schmitz

INTRODUCTION

Virtually every father knows what a "good dad" should do and be. Equally so, virtually every person can use an occasional reminder of what it is he knows to be good, just, and true. *God's Little Devotional Book for Dads* serves as such a reminder.

In this book, you'll find short, to-the-point illustrations and stories that sometimes explain, sometimes amuse, and sometimes hit hard. They are linked to quotations—both familiar and new—and to passages of Scripture, so that each devotional provides a message that is both timely and timeless. In many cases, you'll find these devotionals provide excellent anecdotes to share with your children. And on those occasions in which you are asked to lead a devotional time— perhaps for an organization to which you or one of your children belong—you'll find this book a ready reference for sharing a brief message that is meaningful and memorable.

The Word of God gives us the principle for acquiring God's truth in our lives: "For precept must be upon precept, precept upon precept; line upon line, line upon line; here a little, and there a little" (Isaiah 28:10). *God's Little Devotional Book for Dads*—guaranteed to provide insight and inspiration to fathers everywhere!

THERE ARE MANY WAYS TO MEASURE SUCCESS; NOT THE LEAST OF WHICH IS THE WAY YOUR CHILD DESCRIBES YOU WHEN TALKING TO A FRIEND.

Two little boys were discussing their lives one day, including the various behavioral patterns of their parents. One boy finally asked, "Does your Daddy sit in the den a lot after he comes home from work?"

"No," his friend replied, "he growls all over the place at our house."

Your children not only have a candid opinion about you, but they are also likely to copy your behavior, both good and bad. Even if your child doesn't particularly like what you do—when asked objectively about it—he or she is likely to behave in the same way, unconsciously. A two-year-old might walk with a swagger . . . just like Dad. A three-year-old is likely to use all the words his parents use, even the ones inappropriate for polite company! Above all, children imitate the way their parents behave one to the other.

Three little girls were playing house one day, taking turns playing various roles, when one of them said to another, "Now you be the daddy." The little girl pouted for a minute and then said, "I don't want to be the daddy. I want to talk, and besides, what would I use for a remote control?"

Listen to your children. You may hear an echo!

A child's glory is his father.

PROVERBS 17:6B TLB

A YOUNG SUCCESSFUL ATTORNEY SAID:
THE GREATEST GIFT I EVER RECEIVED WAS A GIFT I GOT ONE CHRISTMAS WHEN MY DAD GAVE ME A SMALL BOX. INSIDE WAS A NOTE SAYING, "SON, THIS YEAR I WILL GIVE YOU 365 HOURS, AN HOUR EVERY DAY AFTER DINNER." MY DAD NOT ONLY KEPT HIS PROMISE, HE SAID, BUT EVERY YEAR HE RENEWED IT AND IT'S THE GREATEST GIFT I EVER HAD IN MY LIFE. I AM THE RESULT OF HIS TIME.

Young Tom attended the best schools Augusta offered, but he always considered his real instructor to be his father. Long before the age when most boys are studying, young Tom was receiving from his father an education that was highly varied, extremely practical, and exceptionally sound academically.

Father and son were near-constant companions, but Sunday afternoons were especially devoted for young Tom's training. While Tom sat on the floor or reclined against an inverted chair, his father—a parson by profession—would pour into Tom's spellbound ears the tales of his own experience, learning, and thought. Tom's father was a man of in-depth information on the affairs of the world, literature, and theology. He coupled a robust imagination with an ability to reason clearly and focus on facts.

Tom eventually earned a doctorate of his own and became president of Princeton University. He also was elected governor of New Jersey. By the time he was elected President of the United States and became the foremost architect of the League of Nations, he had dropped entirely the use of his first name, Thomas. We know him in history simply as Woodrow Wilson— perhaps the most highly educated president in the history of our nation.

You don't need to show your child the world in order to be a great father. You only need to show him the best of your world.

There fore be careful how you walk, not as unwise men, but as wise, making the most of your time . . .

EPHESIANS 5:15-16 NAS

HOW TO CURB JUVENILE
DELINQUENCY:

1. TAKE TIME WITH YOUR
CHILDREN.
2. SET YOUR CHILDREN A GOOD
EXAMPLE.
3. GIVE YOUR CHILDREN IDEALS
FOR LIVING.
4. HAVE A LOT OF ACTIVITIES
PLANNED.
5. DISCIPLINE YOUR CHILDREN.
6. TEACH THEM ABOUT GOD.

M any a parent has moaned with regard to their children who are young adults and away from home: "I did everything I knew to do to be a good parent, and it looks as if nothing has worked." In fact, the good seeds that the parents have sown are still planted deep in the soil of the child's life. It's at this point that the parent must turn to the only thing he or she can do effectively: pray!

Pray daily. Pray persistently. Pray specifically. And above all, pray with faith that God not only hears, but will answer.

A man once said to his friend, "I believe if you thought the Lord told you to jump through a stone wall, you'd jump." The friend replied, "If the Lord told me to jump through a wall, it would be my business to jump, and it would be His business to make a hole."

The same goes for parenting. The Lord tells us to do our part—to raise our children up according to His commandments and to the best of the knowledge we have—and then we must trust Him to do His part in our children's lives.

You can sow, but only God can grow. Trust Him to do that work in your child's life today—to bring to life that which is lying dormant, and to cause your child to grow and flourish into the fullness of the stature of Christ Jesus!

Train up a child in the way he should go: and when he is old, he will not depart from it.

PROVERBS 22:6

"DO YOU REMEMBER YOUR FATHER?" ASKED THE JUDGE STERNLY, "THAT FATHER WHOM YOU HAVE DISGRACED?" THE PRISONER ANSWERED: "I REMEMBER HIM PERFECTLY. WHEN I WENT TO HIM FOR ADVICE OR COMPANIONSHIP, HE WOULD LOOK UP FROM HIS BOOK ON THE LAW OF TRUSTS, AND SAY, 'RUN AWAY, BOY, I AM BUSY' MY FATHER FINISHED HIS BOOK AND HERE I AM."

Albert's father, one of the busiest architects in Mannheim, regarded architecture as merely a means to a financial end. He told a visitor: "It made no difference to me what I did. My main concern was to make money." His money gave young Albert all the material privileges a young boy might imagine: a fourteen-room apartment, servants, a chauffeur, a nanny. Young Albert, however, received neither affection nor understanding from his parents.

Little Albert felt lonely in the family of five. When he began public high school in Heidelberg, two of his new friends quickly encouraged him into mischief. Albert's heart swelled with pride whenever his name was entered in the class book because of some prank he had pulled, and he punctiliously noted the event in his own pocket calendar.

At age 18, despite a brilliance in and love for mathematics, Albert decided to follow his father's advice and study architecture, no doubt hoping to "earn" his father's love in this way. Ten years later, his study was richly rewarded when he gained the unrestricted affection of someone who became a "surrogate" father figure to him: the Fuhrer and Chancellor of the German Reich.

It was not only in architecture that Albert Speer earned Hitler's regard. He became Hitler's Minister of Armaments and War Production, a job in which he had only one goal in mind: to earn "marks" in history's book.

And, ye fathers, provoke not your children to wrath: but bring then up in the nurture and admonition of the Lord.

EPHESIANS 6:4

THE WAY EACH DAY
WILL LOOK TO YOU
ALL STARTS WITH
WHO YOU'RE
LOOKING TO.

A young man was learning to plow with a tractor. He climbed onto the seat of the tractor for his first "solo run," pulled the lever that dropped the plow to the ground, and started across the field. After he had gone a few yards, he turned around to look at the furrow he was making. He became entranced by the rushing flow of topsoil along the plowshare—the rich, black soil turning over in a seemingly endless ribbon. By the time he turned back to see where he was going, he realized that the wheel of the tractor had swerved a number of times. Glancing again behind him, he saw a wavering furrow, a permanent etching into the earth of his wandering eye.

The secret to pulling a straight furrow is not in watching the furrow as it is made, but to set one's sights across the field at a distant point, and to keep the nose of the tractor moving squarely toward that point. The point on which the eyes are fixed must be a fixed point, such as a tree, barn, or hilltop. Only the occasional brief backward glance is allowable!

The same holds true for our life of faith. We are to keep our eyes fixed upon Jesus, who never changes, and to line up our behavior with His Word, looking back only rarely on our ministry and outreach efforts.

Every day you make choices of how you will spend your time and on what you will focus. Be sure you focus on building a relationship with your child.

I will lift up mine eyes unto the hills, from whence cometh my help. My help cometh from the Lord, which made heaven and earth.

PSALM 121:1-2

THE GREATEST
THING A FATHER
CAN DO FOR HIS
CHILDREN IS TO
LOVE THEIR
MOTHER.

A teaching that has resurfaced frequently in the history of the Christian Church is this:

• A child deduces his basic concept of God based upon the image of his own father—the human father is seen as a reflection of the Heavenly Father.

• A child draws his basic concept of the Church based upon the example of his own mother—her daily practical nurturing, teaching, admonishing, and disciplining are internalized by the child as a reflection of these same spiritual qualities provided by the Church.

• A child draws his understanding of how God relates to the Church—and thus, how God relates to him as a member of the Church—by watching how his father relates to his mother, and she to him.

Your example of how you treat your wife is a living parable to your children about how God wants to relate to them! Are you available to your wife? Do you praise and support her? Are you helpful to her? Do you provide for her?

Ask yourself today, "Do I treat my wife as I hope the Lord will treat me?"

So ought men to love their wives as their own bodies. He that loveth his wife loveth himself.

EPHESIANS 5:28

IF YOU WANT YOUR CHILD TO ACCEPT YOUR VALUES WHEN HE REACHES HIS TEEN YEARS, THEN YOU MUST BE WORTHY OF HIS RESPECT DURING HIS YOUNGER DAYS.

Louisa May Alcott not only accepted her parents' values . . . but perpetuated them! She grew up in an extremely generous home even though life was bare in their house, which didn't even have a stove. A friend once observed that their extremely plain and meager meals were often reduced from three a day to two if there was a family who might be in need. The Alcotts themselves, however, would have been the last to consider themselves poor or feel sorry for themselves.

Louisa was once invited to visit, by herself, in Providence. With no other children in the house, she became bored after a few days. She found some dirty, ragged children who seemed to her ideal playmates and she played with them for a long time in the barn. Finding them poorly fed and hungry, she ran in haste to the pantry, which was unguarded at the time, and helped herself to figs and cakes for all. When her hostess discovered what she had done, she scolded her soundly and sent her to the attic to ponder her outrageous behavior. Dear Louisa. She didn't have the faintest idea that "feeding the poor" was wrong. She was later found not crying or the least bit repentant, but rather, angry that her hostess had not also offered more for her to take to her new friends!

. . . a model for you, that you might follow our example.

2 THESSALONIANS 3:9 NAS

A CHILD IS NOT LIKELY TO FIND A FATHER IN GOD UNLESS HE FINDS SOMETHING OF GOD IN HIS FATHER.

Jim, an elder at a church, was assigned to oversee the evangelism of a group of Vietnamese refugees who had just moved into the church's neighborhood. He felt especially drawn to Sun Lee and his family, who had no I possessions, knew no one, and needed help in every way. Jim began by helping the family get food and then he helped Sun Lee find a job.

Jim wanted so much to tell Sun Lee about Jesus Christ, but since he didn't speak Vietnamese and the refugees knew very little English, he found it difficult to communicate. Both Jim and Sun Lee began to learn as much of each other's language as possible so they could become better friends.

One day Jim felt that he finally knew enough Vietnamese to tell Sun Lee about Jesus, but the more he talked, the more confused Sun Lee seemed to be. Finally, Sun Lee blurted out, "Is your God like you?"

Jim replied, "Oh, He's far, far greater."

Sun Lee interrupted, "If He's like you, Jim, I want to I know Him."

The most effective communication you can speak is the "word" of your deeds.

Be ye followers of me, even as I also am of Christ.

1 CORINTHIANS 11:1

A FATHER'S WORDS ARE LIKE A THERMOSTAT THAT SETS THE TEMPERATURE IN THE HOUSE.

We've all no doubt heard the popular phrase, "You're talking so loud I can't hear you." An old poem confirms that good advice about "taming the tongue" has been offered by virtually every culture, tribe, and race!

"The boneless tongue, so small and weak,
Can crush and kill," declares the Greek.
"The tongue destroys a greater horde,"
The Turk asserts, "than does the sword."
The Persian proverb wisely saith,
"A lengthy tongue—an early death!"
Or sometimes takes this form instead,
"Don't let your tongue cut off your head."
"The tongue can speak a word whose speed,"
Say the Chinese, "outstrips the steed."
The Arab sages said in part,
"The tongue's great storehouse is the heart."
From Hebrew was the maxim sprung,
"Thy feet should slip, but ne'er the tongue."
The sacred writer crowns the whole,
"Who keeps the tongue doth keep his soul."

The solution to the arms race . . . rising rates of crime, abuse, and divorce . . . may very well lie . . . in the tongue.

Death and life are in the power of the tongue: and they that love it shall eat the fruit thereof

PROVERBS 18:21

WHILE I DON'T MINIMIZE THE VITAL ROLE PLAYED BY A MOTHER, I BELIEVE SUCCESSFUL FAMILY BEGINS WITH HER HUSBAND.

In their classic book *Cheaper by the Dozen*, Frank B. Gilbreth, Jr., and Ernestine Gilbreth Carey describe their father as a man who "always practiced what he preached, and it was just about impossible to tell where his scientific management company ended and his family life began. His office was always full of children, and he often took two or three of us, and sometimes all twelve, on business trips . . .

"On the other hand, our house at Montclair, New Jersey, was a sort of school for scientific management and the elimination of wasted motions."

Gilbreth installed work charts in the bathrooms, took moving pictures of his children doing chores to help identify wasted motion, and insisted that a child who wanted extra pocket money submit a sealed bid, with the lowest bidder getting the contract. Still, his children didn't seem to mind their regimented life. Why? Primarily because Dad "had a respect for them, too, and didn't mind showing it." He believed about children that "there's no limit to what you can teach. Really, it was a love of children more than anything else that made him want a pack of his own."

It's not the rules that a father exacts that cause a child to rebel, but rather, a lack of love and respect.

He must be one who manages his own household well, keeping his children under control with all dignity.

1 TIMOTHY 3:4 NAS

HAPPY IS THE CHILD WHO HAPPENS IN UPON HIS PARENT FROM TIME TO TIME TO SEE HIM ON HIS KNEES, . . . OR GOING ASIDE REGULARLY, TO KEEP TIMES WITH THE LORD.

"You must have a good heart," one man said to his child, "if you are going to act right in this world." And then in illustrating his point he continued, "Suppose my watch was not keeping time very well. Would it do any good if I went to the town clock, and made the hands of my watch point exactly the same as those of the larger clock in the square? No, of course not! Soon my watch would be just as inaccurate as before. Rather, I should take my watch to a watchmaker, or to a jewelry store that repairs watches. It is only when my watch has been cleaned and repaired that its hands will be able to keep time accurately all day long."

When we spend time in prayer, we are, in like manner, going to the Heart Maker, asking Him to "clean and repair our hearts" from the damage caused by sins we have committed. We are asking Him to put us right again on the inside, so that we can more clearly discern right from wrong. When our children see us doing this, they are much more likely to go to the Heart Maker when they feel their own lives in disarray or "out of sync"—rather than turn to

If the world and reset their souls according to its standards and priorities.

...let the heart of them rejoice that seek the Lord, seek the Lord, and his strength: seek his face evermore.

PSALM 105:3-4

WHEN GOD
MEASURES A MAN,
HE PUTS THE TAPE
AROUND THE HEART
INSTEAD OF THE
HEAD.

A s he was returning home from the Capitol one evening, Senator John Stennis was robbed at gunpoint. Even though Stennis turned over what little of value he was carrying, the robbers shot him twice, hitting him in the stomach and leg. The surgeons at Walter Reed Medical Center labored for more than six hours to repair the damage and save his life.

Also on his way home that evening was Senator Mark Hatfield, who had clashed often and sharply with Stennis. The two were at virtually opposite ends of the political spectrum. However, when Hatfield heard on his car radio what had happened, he immediately drove to the hospital. There, he quickly discerned that the switchboard staff was overwhelmed with the many incoming calls from Stennis' fellow senators, reporters, and friends. He said to an operator, "I know how to work one of these; let me help you out." He helped answer phones until daylight when the calls subsided. Then, without fanfare, he quietly introduced himself as he was leaving, "My name is Hatfield . . . happy to help out on behalf of a man I deeply respect."

"Bigness" means being free of pettiness, grudges, vengeance, and prejudice. It means caring unconditionally, helping unassumingly.

. . . for the Lord seeth not as man seeth; for man looketh on the outward appearance, but the Lord looketh on the heart.

1 SAMUEL 16:7

O LORD BUILD ME A SON WHOSE HEART WILL BE CLEAR, WHOSE GOAL WILL BE HIGH, A SON WHO WILL MASTER HIMSELF BEFORE HE SEEKS TO MASTER OTHER MEN; ONE WHO WILL REACH INTO THE FUTURE, YET NEVER FORGET THE PAST.

Thomas J. Watson, Jr., writes in *Father, Son & Co.—My life at IBM and Beyond* about his first days as CEO: "When my father died in 1956—six weeks after making me head of IBM—I was the most frightened man in America. For ten years he had groomed me to succeed him, and I had been the young man in a hurry, eager to take over, cocky and impatient. Now, suddenly, I had the job—but what I didn't have was Dad there to back me up."

Watson admits that he "didn't have much motivation as a youth." He was neither student nor athlete. At Brown University, he spent so much time flying airplanes that he barely graduated. His father encouraged him, however, saying, "At some point, something will catch hold and you are going to be a great man." After World War II, Watson returned home "confident, for the first time, that I might be capable of running IBM." And he did! During his 15 years as head of IBM, the company entered the computer era and grew more than tenfold, becoming a $7.5 billion-a-year business. He says of the success, "I think I was at least successful enough that people could say I was the worthy son of a worthy father."

A wise son brings joy to his father . . .

PROVERBS 10:1 NIV

TOO MUCH LOVE
NEVER SPOILS
CHILDREN.
CHILDREN BECOME
SPOILED WHEN WE
SUBSTITUTE
"PRESENTS" FOR
"PRESENCE."

A man once gave his little boy a baseball and a baseball bat . . . but he never pitched the ball to his son or showed him how to swing the bat. He gave his boy a toy gun . . . but he never showed him how to play "cop" with it, instead of robber.

A man once gave his son a pocket knife . . . but he never showed him how to use it to carve an animal from a bar of soap. He gave his boy a BB-gun . . . but he never took him to a firing range to show him how to use it safely or took him along on his hunting trips.

The man was astonished the day two police-men came to his door with a tale about his boy and others in the neighborhood who had formed a malicious gang. "Not my son," he said. "I've never taught him violence."

"Perhaps not," the policeman answered. "But in the shed that the boys were using for their headquarters, we found clubs, guns, and knives."

"Perhaps," the other policeman added, "You didn't teach your son how *not* to be violent."

Never expect your child to understand the world from the things you give to him. He needs for you to show him what to expect in life, how to embrace life, and to live life to its fullest.

We loved you dearly—so dearly that we gave you not only God's message, but our own lives too.

1 THESSALONIANS 2:8 TLB

LIVE TRUTH
INSTEAD OF
PROFESSING IT.

A reporter once asked Sam Rayburn, who was Speaker of the House of Representatives at the time:

"Mr. Speaker, you see at least a hundred people a day. You tell each one yes or no. You never seem to make notes on what you have told them, but I have never heard of your forgetting anything you have promised them. What is your secret?"

Rayburn's eyes flashed as he answered, "If you tell the truth the first time, you don't have to remember."

Truth extends to honesty. If you are honest in all of your dealings, you never have to remember whom you may have cheated.

Truth extends to positive encouragement. If you speak a good truth of all people, you never have to avoid anybody.

Truth spills over into the "implied." If you refuse to give false impressions, you never need to cover up.

And truth extends to the exaggeration, the innuendo, and the implication. If you refrain from twisting the truth, you never need to unravel a relationship gone awry.

But be ye doers of the word, and not hearers only, deceiving your own selves.

JAMES 1:22

IMPOSSIBILITIES VANISH WHEN A MAN AND HIS GOD CONFRONT A MOUNTAIN.

Walking on the moon was once considered to be fry impossible, and yet Neil Armstrong and Buzz Aldrin did just that on July 20, 1969. Michael Collins, the astronaut who remained aloft in *Columbia*, writes of another seeming impossibility overcome that day:

"They hadn't been out on the surface very long when the three of us got a big surprise. The President of the United States began talking on the radio! Mr. Nixon said, 'Neil and Buzz, I am talking to you by telephone from the Oval Office at the White House, and this certainly has to be the most historic telephone call ever made . . . Because of what you have done, the heavens have become a part of man's world. As you talk to us from the Sea of Tranquility, it inspires us to redouble our efforts to bring peace and tranquility to Earth.'"

Our prayers are like an unseen communication link that spans heaven and earth. Things once regarded as impossible become possible when that link is firmly established.

. . . but with God all things are possible.

MATTHEW 19:26

FOR MANY LITTLE GIRLS, LIFE WITH FATHER IS DRESS REHEARSAL FOR LOVE AND MARRIAGE.

n one of his short stories, O. Henry tells of an only child whose mother had died. Her father would come home from work, fix their meal, and then sit down with his paper and pipe, put his feet up on the hassock, and read. When the little girl, starved for companionship after being home alone all day, would ask, "Father, would you play with me?" he would reply, "No, I'm too tired" or, "No, I'm too busy." He usually advised her, "Go out on the street and play."

This little girl heard her father's advice to go out on the street and play so often that she literally grew up on the streets outside her home. She eventually became a streetwalker, a prostitute—to her dying day, she continued to search on the streets for affection and someone with whom to keep company.

Neglect is one of the most devastating ways a parent can abuse a child. Tell your child that you love her, and spend time with her so she won't have to find someone else who will.

Those things, which ye have both learned, and received, and heard, and seen in me, do: and the God of peace shall be with you.

PHILIPPIANS 4:9

MY PRIMARY ROLE IS NOT TO BE THE BOSS AND JUST LOOK GOOD BUT TO BE A SERVANT LEADER WHO ENABLES AND ENHANCES MY FAMILY TO BE THEIR BEST.

During the Civil War, the son of a Quaker family in Pennsylvania left home against his father's wishes and enlisted in the cause of the North. Time passed and no word was heard from him. One night the father had a dream that his son was in great need. The next morning the father left the farm and after discovering where the troops had been sent, made his way by horse-drawn buggy to the battlefield. In asking about his son, he learned that the troops had been under heavy fire earlier in the day and many had fallen wounded. The father asked for permission to try to find his son, and the commander wearily granted it.

The father searched late into the afternoon and when it was dark, he lit a lantern and went from person to person, letting the light fall across the faces of the wounded young men. As he stumbled among the bodies, he began calling loudly after every few steps, "Jonathan Smythe, thy father a seeketh after thee." Diligently, he kept at his search until finally, he heard a very faint, barely audible reply, "Father, over here." And then he added, "I knew you would come."

Can your child count on you to find him when he is in distress and come to his aid? A true servant always looks for a way to help and give comfort.

Let this mind be in you, which was also in Christ Jesus: . . . (who) took upon him the form of a servant . . .

PHILIPPIANS 2:5,7

WE TOO OFTEN LOVE THINGS AND USE PEOPLE, WHEN WE SHOULD BE USING THINGS AND LOVING PEOPLE.

When Andrew Carnegie sold his steel company in 1901, his share of the sale price ensured that he would receive $1 million a month, for life. What did he do with the money? He gave it away!

During the last eighteen years of his life, Carnegie gave away nearly $350 million. He believed that the lives of rich men are divided into two parts: the first for getting money, the second for giving it away. He also believed that rich men could make a better world, and he focused his giving very specifically. He helped pay for 2,800 libraries in the United States and the British Empire, at a cost of $60 million. Carnegie believed that children like himself could improve their minds by reading, even if they could not stay in school very long. He gave $30 million to American and British universities, mostly to smaller schools, because he wanted the children of poor workers to have a chance for a college & education. He also gave large amounts of money for pensions for teachers and steelworkers. And, he made possible the Carnegie Hero Fund, which gave awards for bravery in time of peace.

Carnegie truly was a man who used what he had earned to show love to others.

Be devoted to one another in brotherly love. Honor one another above yourselves.

ROMANS 12:10 NIV

THE KIND OF MAN WHO THINKS THAT HELPING WITH THE DISHES IS BENEATH HIM WILL ALSO THINK THAT HELPING WITH THE BABY IS BENEATH HIM, AND THEN HE CERTAIN IS NOT GOING TO BE A VERY SUCCESSFUL FATHER.

The great Protestant reformer Martin Luther once wrote this about the role of a husband and father: "Along comes the clever harlot, namely natural reason, looks at married life, turns up her nose and says: 'Why must I rock the baby, wash its diapers, change its bed, smell its odor, heal its rash, take care of this and take care of that, do this and do that? It is better to remain single and live a quiet and carefree life. I will become a priest or a nun and tell my children to do the same.'

"But what does the Christian faith say? The father opens his eyes, looks at these lowly, distasteful, and despised things and knows that they are adorned with divine approval as with the most precious gold and silver. God, with His angels and creatures, will smile—not because diapers are washed, but because it is done in faith."

Even the most mundane task can become an act of "worship"—an act of service rendered not to others, but as unto God. As you help your wife and children with the simplest of chores, imagine that you are doing the task for the benefit of the Lord Jesus Himself.

. . . but whoever wishes to become great among you shall be your servant.

MATTHEW 20:26 NAS

THE BEST
THINGS YOU
GIVE CHILDREN,
NEXT TO GOOD
HABITS, ARE
GOOD
MEMORIES.

The two boys were dressed and ready to go. In fact, they had been ready for more than an hour. Excitement flooded their faces and all their talk was about only one thing: their father had promised to take them to the circus that afternoon!

As planned, Dad came home from work after lunch and quickly changed into casual clothing. Then, just as the three of them were about to leave the house, the phone rang. The boys listened as their father talked with the person on the other end of the line. Bit by bit, their faces began to fall. This was obviously a business call, and some urgent matter was requiring their father's attention downtown. Disappointment rolled into the room like a dark cloud. Their mother also overheard what she thought was the inevitable change of plans. And then, to the surprise of all, they heard Dad say, "No, I won't be down. It will just have to wait until morning."

Hanging up the phone he called for the boys to meet him at the car as he turned to kiss his wife good-bye. She smiled and with a twinge of fear that he may have made the wrong decision, she said, "The circus keeps coming back, you know." The father replied, "Yes, I know. But childhood doesn't."

The memory of the righteous is blessed . . .

PROVERBS 10:7 NAS

HONOR IS BETTER THAN HONORS.

F rancis I, King of France from 1515-1547, spent some 27 years of his reign at war with Charles V, the German Emperor and King of Spain. The hostility began in 1521 and two years later, while Francis was pursuing his enemies, he received word that his wife had died. Shortly thereafter, he received notice that his second daughter had also died.

During the battle of Pavia in 1525, Francis was defeated, wounded, and taken prisoner. In a letter to his mother from prison, he wrote, "Madame, to inform you of the rest of my misfortune, I have nothing left to me save my honour and my life."

The Emperor demanded one-third of France, renunciation of France's claim to Italy, and the return of Charles de Bourbon's provinces, along with Provence. Francis did the honorable thing and refused, saying, "I am resolved to endure prison for as long as God wills rather than accept terms injurious to my kingdom." Francis retained honor to the end, not only for himself, but for all Frenchmen.

There may be times in our lives when all we have left is our honor and our lives. Even so, that is sufficient, for honor transcends life itself. It passes into history even as we pass into eternity.

. . . for them that honor me, I will honor . . .

1 SAMUEL 2:30

IT MAY BE HARD ON SOME FATHERS NOT TO HAVE A SON, BUT IT IS MUCH HARDER ON A BOY NOT TO HAVE A FATHER.

A very successful Christian businessman had one son. He was very proud of this boy, who seemed to have grown to be a well-educated and well-respected gentleman. Then one day, the son was arrested for embezzlement and upon trial, was found guilty. All through the trial and up to the rendering of the verdict, the young man appeared unconcerned and nonchalant. He seemed more proud than humbled or broken by the experience.

Then the verdict was brought in. The judge told the young man to stand for the sentence, which he did—still somewhat cocky in demeanor. He glanced around the courtroom and to his amazement he saw that his father was also standing. His father had realized that he, too, was involved—not with what the boy had done, but with what the boy had become.

The young man saw his father—an honest man with a clear conscience—bowed low with sorrow and shame to receive, as though it were for himself, his son's sentence. The son wept bitterly, and for the first time, truly repented of his crime.

The future of a boy cannot be separated from the present—or the presence—of his father.

Withhold not good from them to whom it is due, when it is in the power of thine hand to do it.

PROVERBS 3:27

IT IS NOT WHAT A MAN DOES THAT DETERMINES WHETHER HIS WORK IS SACRED OR SECULAR, IT IS WHY HE DOES IT.

L egend has it that a missionary was swept overboard while traveling on very high and rough seas, and was subsequently washed up on a beach at the edge of a remote native village. Nearly dead from exposure and lack of food and fresh water, he was found by the people of the village and nursed back to health. He lived among them for twenty years, quietly adapting to their culture and working alongside them. He preached no sermons, and made no personal faith claim. He neither read nor recited Scripture to them.

But . . . when people were sick, he sat with them, sometimes all night. When people were hungry, he fed them. When people were lonely, he gave a listening ear. He taught the ignorant and always took the side of the one who had been wronged.

The day came when missionaries entered this village and began talking to the people about a man named Jesus. After listening for awhile to their story, the native people began insisting that Jesus had already been living in their village for many years. "Come," one of them said, "we'll intro- duce you to Him." The missionaries were led to a hut where they found their long-lost companion!

Why we work always determines *how* we live.

Whatever you do, work at it with all your heart, as working for the Lord, not for men . . . It is the Lord Christ you are serving.

COLOSSIANS 3:23-24 NIV

THE MOST
EFFECTIVE THING
WE CAN DO FOR OUR
CHILDREN AND
FAMILIES IS PRAY
FOR THEM.

Spiritual giants in every age have agreed about prayer: more is better. The founder of Methodism, John Wesley, spent one to two hours a day in private communication with God. Both Martin Luther and Bishop Francis Asbury believed two hours of prayer a day was a minimum. The great Scottish preacher John Welch regularly prayed eight to ten hours a day—and then often awoke in the middle of the night to continue his conversation with the Lord.

None of these men were ivory-tower contemplatives with nothing else to do. Asbury, for example, traveled some 300,000 miles, mostly on horseback, to build the American Methodist Church. All advocated that a person combine prayer with work, including praying *as* one works.

Today, many parents lead such busy lives they often think they have no time for prayer on behalf of their families. Yet, the most potent thing a parent can do is to pray. As you drive to work, walk from place to place, do mundane chores . . . talk to God at length about each child. Thank God for your children. Listen for His advice. The change in your child and your relationship with your child is likely to be remarkable, even miraculous!

Devote yourselves to prayer, keeping alert in it with an attitude of thanksgiving.

COLOSSIANS 4:2 NAS

A FATHER SHOULD NEVER MAKE DISTINCTIONS BETWEEN HIS CHILDREN.

A Sunday school superintendent was registering two new boys in Sunday school. She asked their ages and birthdays so she could place them in the appropriate classes. The bolder of the two replied, "We're both seven. My birthday is April 8 and my brother's birthday is April 20." The superintendent replied, "But that's not possible, boys." The quieter brother spoke up. "No, it's true. One of us is adopted."

"Oh?" asked the superintendent, not convinced. "Which one?" The two brothers looked at each other and smiled. The bolder one said, "We asked Dad that same question awhile ago, but he just looked at us and said he loved us both equally, and he couldn't remember anymore which one of us was adopted."

What a wonderful analogy of God's love! The Apostle Paul wrote to the Romans: "Now if we are [God's] children, then we are heirs—heirs of God and co-heirs with Christ . . ." (Romans 8:17, NIV). In essence, as adopted sons and daughters of God, we fully share in the inheritance of His begotten Son, Jesus. If our Heavenly Father can love us on ! equal footing with His beloved Son, surely we can love our children equally and show no partiality in the blessings—or privileges—we extend to them.

For them is no respect of persons with God.

ROMANS 2:11

CHARACTER IS
WHAT YOU ARE
IN THE DARK.

A nurse named Carol was once the victim of an elaborate hoax. A con artist came to her claiming to know a famous rock star. He asked the nurse to loan him her car so he could bring the rock star from a nearby auditorium to visit the quadriplegic children and adults under her care. He was so convincing and gave so many details that Carol allowed him to take her car. Not only did Carol lose her car, but she lost the respect of many of her patients whom she had told about the impending visit.

When the rock star heard how his name had been misused, he decided to take action. Without media attention, he made a surprise visit to the hospital. He met Carol and with her by his side, he spoke warmly to her patients, signing autographs, passing out copies of his latest recording, and giving away posters as he greeted each one personally.

Nurse Carol said after his visit, "You should have seen the smiles on their faces. He's more than a rock star to them now. He's become their friend."

The "onstage" character played by many people is not the same as the person's backstage persona. It's backstage character that truly counts, however. And in the end, it's the only character worth playing!

The integrity of the upright shall guide them . . .

PROVERBS 11:3

In *A Christmas Carol*, Charles Dickens' character Scrooge rails to his nephew about Christmas: "What's Christmas time . . . but a time for paying bilk without money; a time for finding yourself a year older, and not an hour richer; a time for balancing your books? . . . If I could work my will, every idiot who goes about with 'Merry Christmas,' on his lips, should be boiled with his own pudding, and buried with a stake of holly through his heart. He should!" Scrooge then gives his opinion about his nephew's celebration of Christmas, "Much good it has ever done you!"

At this, Scrooge's nephew replies, "There are many things from which I might have derived good, by which I have not profited, I dare say, Christmas among the rest. But I am sure I have always thought of Christmas time . . . as a good time: a kind, forgiving, charitable, pleasant time: the only time I know of, in the long calendar of the year, when men and women seem by one consent to open their shut-up hearts freely . . . And therefore, uncle, though it has never put a scrap of gold or silver in my pocket, I believe that it has done me good, and will do me good."

The *unseen* reward of making a commitment to Christ *now* does not make it less valuable in eternity!

For what is a man profited, if he shall gain the whole world, and lose his own soul? . . .

MATTHEW 16:26

YOU CANNOT TEACH A CHILD TO TAKE CARE OF HIMSELF UNLESS YOU WILL LET HIM TRY . . . HE WILL MAKE MISTAKES; AND OUT OF THESE MISTAKES WILL COME HIS WISDOM.

Two hunters chartered a plane to fly them into a remote region in Canada so that they might hunt for elk. The plane returned for them a few days later. Indeed, the hunt had been successful—the two hunters had six elk to show for their effort.

When the pilot explained to them that his plane could only carry four of the elk, the hunters protested, "But the plane that we chartered last year was exactly like this one. It had the same horsepower, the weather was similar, and we took out six elk then."

Hearing this, the pilot reluctantly agreed to load all six elk. The plane struggled during takeoff, but was unable to gain sufficient altitude to climb out of the valley. It crashed near the top of a mountain. To their great fortune, all three men survived.

As the hunters stumbled out of the wreckage, one of them asked the dazed pilot, "Do you know where we are?"

He mumbled, "No." The other hunter, however, looked around and said confidently, "I think we're about a mile from where we crashed last year!"

Mistakes are meant to lead to wisdom, not to future error. Teach your child to draw lessons from his skinned knees and bruised elbows. He'll have less pain and fewer scrapes in his adult life.

And all thy children shall be taught of the Lord; and great shall be the peace of thy children.

ISAIAH 54:13

HE WHO SACRIFICES HIS CONSCIENCE TO AMBITION BURNS A PICTURE TO OBTAIN THE ASHES.

Bubba Smith became famous not only for his performance on the football field, but perhaps even more so, for his performances on television as a spokesman for a brewery. The day came, however, when Bubba swore off booze.

Now, Bubba never did drink. Still, he sold countless kegs of beer by making clever beer commercials. He may be the first athlete ever to give up a highly lucrative, easy, and amusing job because he felt it was morally wrong. Why did | he take this step?

Bubba was invited to be the grand marshal of a major university's homecoming parade, and as he rode around the field during halftime, he heard drunken college fans yelling, "Tastes great!" while others shouted, "Less filling." In Bubba's opinion, they should have been yelling, "Go, State!" or, "Get 'em, Bubba."

Bubba Smith realized in a matter of moments that he was encouraging others to do something that he himself chose not to do. When young school children began approaching him on the streets reciting his commercials verbatim, Bubba hung up his commercial career, saying simply, "I had to stop compromising my principles." May a clear conscience always be more valuable to us than man-made rewards!

Holding faith, and a good conscience; which some having put away concerning faith have made shipwreck.

1 TIMOTHY 1:19

n 1955, the black people of Montgomery, Alabama, were angry when Rosa Parks was arrested for sitting in the front of a bus—the area supposedly reserved for w white passengers only. The 27-year-old minister of the B Dexter Avenue Baptist Church in Montgomery met with M other ministers to decide on a course of action. They urged their fellow blacks not to ride the city's buses on December 5. The bus boycott, however, lasted 382 days. The ministers repeatedly urged blacks to remain peaceful and calm.

The publicity surrounding the bus boycott made the young minister, Martin Luther King, Jr., famous internationally, almost overnight. Then he became not only a spokesman, but a target. A bomb exploded on his front porch. Nobody was hurt, but a crowd of more than a thousand blacks gathered in anger. King spoke from the smoking ruins of his porch, saying, "Be peaceful. I want you to love your enemies."

It's one thing to advocate change when you are speaking behind a microphone. It's another to stand for m change when your wife and children barely escape death. But King was a man of deep convictions, and in his standing in crisis, an even stronger message was sent to those who opposed civil rights for blacks.

If thou faint in the day of adversity, thy strength is small.

PROVERBS 24:10

IF YOU TELL THE TRUTH, YOU DON'T HAVE TO REMEMBER ANYTHING.

Four high school boys skipped their first period class one morning in order to joyride around town. Coming in late, they all apologized profusely to the teacher, claiming that they had had a flat tire on the way to school. They gave a long litany of complications they had experienced in repairing it.

The teacher smiled sympathetically, and then explained that they had missed a quiz given during the first period. "Can't we make it up?" one of the boys asked. Another chimed in, "It wasn't our fault." A third added, "Surely you can't hold a flat tire against us."

The teacher said, "Well, all right." She then told the boys to take empty seats in the four corners of the room, to take out paper and pencil, and answer this one question: "Which tire was flat?"

There's no substitute for telling the truth!

Sometimes we think that if we only tell a little "white lie" we really aren't hurting anybody. In fact, we are . . . ourselves . . . for in telling lies of any size we are developing a pattern in our lives of mixing black with white. Eventually we will see only gray, and be unable to discern clearly the truth of what is right and wrong.

A truthful witness gives honest testimony, but a false witness tells lies.

PROVERBS 12:17 NIV

I magine for a moment that your bank suddenly announced this as its new policy:

Every morning your account is going to be credited with $86,400. You can carry no balance from day to day. Every evening, your account will be cancelled and whatever amount of your account you have failed to use during the day will be returned to the bank.

What would you do? Why, you'd draw out every cent of the $86,400 each day, and spend it, save it, or invest it as wisely as possible. Before long, you could be a very wealthy person, indeed!

Actually, you have a bank account with a similar policy. It is called "Time." Every morning, you are given the prospect of 86,400 seconds. At the close of that twenty-four hour period, the moments you have failed to withdraw and invest to good purpose are ruled off your ledger. Time carries no balances from day to day. It allows no overdrafts. Each day, a new account is opened to you. If you fail to withdraw and use the day's deposit, the loss is yours.

Those who truly love life use time to the maximum. They make their days count rather than counting their days!

And I will very gladly spend and be spent for you . . . .

2 CORINTHIANS 12:15

When television journalist Bob Greene was first asked by others how it felt to be a new father, he recalls, "Normally, I shrug the question off; it's so complicated and so consuming that I don't feel I can do it justice with a glib reply. I usually just say, 'Yeah, it's great,' and let it go at that."

One day, however, he truly expressed to two friends how he felt. He writes in his book, *Good Morning, Merry Sunshine*: "I don't even know how to explain it. I've been spending time on the road ever since I started working for a living. I've complained about it a lot, but I've really liked the idea of it. Going into different cities, sleeping in hotels, meeting strange people . . . I've really liked it.

"Now, though, when I'm gone . . . I physically ache for missing my daughter. It never seems that any story is important enough to make me not see her for another day. I know I still go out on the road all the time—I wonder if I'm fooling myself—but missing her is not some vague concept in my mind. It actually hurts when I think that she's at home and I'm not with her. Sometimes I fall asleep thinking about it."

Sometimes the feelings of being a dad are beyond words. And that's okay.

Lo, children are an heritage of the Lord:
and the fruit of the womb is his reward.

PSALM 127:3

TRUST IN YOURSELF AND YOU ARE DOOMED TO DISAPPOINTMENT; . . . . TRUST IN MONEY AND YOU MAY HAVE IT TAKEN FROM YOU . . . BUT TRUST IN GOD, AND YOU ARE NEVER TO BE CONFOUNDED IN TIME OR ETERNITY.

Eight of the most powerful money magnates in the world gathered for a meeting at the Edgewater Beach Hotel in Chicago, Illinois, in 1923. The combined resources and assets of these eight men tallied more than the U.S. Treasury that year. In the group were Charles Schwab, president of a steel company, Richard Whitney, president of the New York Stock Exchange, and Arthur Cutton, a wheat speculator. Albert Fall was a presidential cabinet member, a personally wealthy man. Jesse Livermore was the greatest Wall Street "bear" in his generation. Leon Fraser was the president of the International Bank of Settlements, and Ivan Krueger headed the largest monopoly in the nation. An impressive gathering of financial eagles!

What happened to these men in later years? Schwab died penniless. Whitney served a life sentence in Sing Sing Prison. Cutton became insolvent. Fall was pardoned from a federal prison so he might die at home. Fraser, Livermore, and Krueger committed suicide. Seven of these eight extremely rich men had lives that turned out disastrous.

What a mistake it is to think that you control what you have—be it life or money.

It is better to take refuge in the Lord than to trust in man.

PSALM 118:8 NIV

THE SUPERIOR MAN
. . . STANDS ERECT
BY BENDING ABOVE
THE FALLEN. HE
RISES BY LIFTING
OTHERS.

Andrew Davison had a rare and life-impacting opportunity to visit Dr. Albert Schweitzer at his jungle hospital on the banks of the Ogowe River. For three days, he engaged in leisurely conversation with the great humanitarian, theologian, musician, and physician. He reported later that his three-day visit had a deep and profound effect on him. In writing of his visit, however, Davison didn't relay the content of their conversations, but rather, this incident:

"It was about eleven in the morning. The equatorial sun was beating down mercilessly, and we were walking up a hill with Dr. Schweitzer. Suddenly he left us and strode across the slope of the hill to a place where an African woman was struggling upward with a huge armload of wood for the cook-fires. I watched with both admiration and concern as the eighty-five-year-old man took the entire load of wood and carried it on up the hill for the relieved woman. When we all reached the top of the hill, one of the members of our group asked Dr. Schweitzer why he did things like that, implying that in that heat and at his age he should not. Albert Schweitzer, looking right at all of us and pointing to the woman, said simply, 'No one should ever have to carry a burden like that alone.'"

And we urge you, brethren, admonish the unruly, encourage the fainthearted, help the weak, be patient with all men.

1 THESSALONIANS 5:14 NAS

CHILDREN
SPELL "LOVE"

. . .

T-I-M-E.

Every time baseball player Tim Burke left to go on the road, he found it more difficult to leave his wife and their three children. Stephanie, age 4, confessed to her father why she was upset one day, "You go away all the time to play baseball." Though he did his best to console her, he felt as if he was consoling himself.

When spring training rolled around the next year, Tim's heart wasn't in it. He asked his wife, "How would you feel about my retiring?" Although his wife was scared he might regret the decision, especially since baseball was Tim's first and only job, she also was scared at the toll another season might have on their family. By the second week of spring training, however, Tim had reached a decision. He announced to his manager, "I've decided to retire today."

After he had cleared out his locker, reporters gathered around to ask, "Why?" Tim gave this eloquent answer: "My family needs me more than the Reds do. Baseball's going to do just fine without me, but I'm the only father my children have. I'm the only husband my wife has. And they need me now."

Many men dream of living the life of a professional ball player. Tim Burke gave it up for the life he dreamed about.

Don't befools; be wise; make the most of every opportunity you have for doing good.

EPHESIANS 5:16 TLB

IT IS BETTER TO BIND YOUR CHILDREN TO YOU BY A FEELING OF RESPECT, AND BY GENTLENESS, THAN BY FEAR.

A mother and her children went looking for a Father's Day card one year. Suddenly, the youngest of the four children shouted with glee, "I found it! I found it!" After each of the children had read the card, they passed it to Mom with an unanimous vote—and fortunately, a laugh: "This is it, Mom! This is for Dad."

The woman took the card and saw that it had been written to indicate a small child's block printing. On the front of the card was a little boy with dirty sneakers. They were untied, naturally. His cap was twisted to one side, his jeans were torn. He obviously was dirty and sweaty from playing hard outside. He was holding on to the handle of a little wagon, loaded with broken toys and a baseball bat. In his hip pocket was a sling shot. His eye was black, and he had a Band-Aid stuck on his arm. The front of the card read: "Dad, I'll never forget that little prayer you said for me every day." And then on the inside of the card were these words: "God help you if you ever do that again!"

Discipline your child as a display of power, and they'll fear you . . . and eventually distrust you . . . and then hate you. Discipline your child out of love and with love, however, and they'll respect you for it.

. . . thy gentleness hath made me great.

PSALM 18:35

THE BEST TIME FOR YOU TO HOLD YOUR TONGUE IS THE TIME YOU FEEL YOU MUST SAY SOMETHING OR BUST.

M any analogies have been given for the "untamed tongue." Quarles likened it to a drawn sword that takes a person prisoner: "A word unspoken is like the sword in the scabbard, thine; if vented, thy sword is in another's hand."

Others have described evil-speaking as:

· *a freezing wind*—one that seals up the sparkling waters and kills the tender flowers and shoots of growth. In similar fashion, bitter and hate-filled words bind up the hearts of men and cause love to cease to flourish.

· *a fox with a firebrand tied to its tail*, sent out among the standing corn just as in the days of Samson and the Philistines. So gossip spreads without control or reason.

· *a pistol fired in the mountains*, the echo of which is intensified until it sounds like thunder.

· *a snowball that gathers size* as it rolls down a mountain.

Perhaps the greatest analogy, however, is one given by a little child who came running to her parent in tears. "Did your friend hurt you?" the parent asked.

"Yes," said the girl. "Where?" the parent asked again.

"Right here," said the child, pointing to her heart.

Don't talk so much. You keep putting your foot in your mouth. Be sensible and turn off the flow!

PROVERBS 10:19 TLB

LAUGHTER IS THE SHORTEST DISTANCE BETWEEN TWO PEOPLE.

One day Dr. Bernie S. Siegel, author of *Peace, Love, and Healing*, got a call from a policeman friend, who began talking about all of the horrors in the world and about the despair of his own life. He finally said morbidly, "I have nothing to live for. I just called to say good-bye."

"Good-bye?" asked Siegel. "What do you mean?"

The friend said in a monotone voice, "I'm going to commit suicide. I just called to say good-bye."

Without a pause, Siegel quipped, "Well, if you do, I'll never speak to you again."

Astounded—and jolted from his deep malaise—the policeman started to chuckle. Instead of shooting himself as he had planned, he decided to go see his friend Bernie for a heart-to-heart chat.

It's very, very difficult to remain angry at someone who makes you laugh. It's hard to remain sad around a person who makes you giggle. It's extremely difficult to hold a grudge against a person who brings a smile to your face. It's almost impossible to stay frightened if you're with a person who causes you to chuckle.

Laughter is a tie that binds hearts together.

The light in the eyes [of him whose heart is joyful] rejoices the hearts of others.

PROVERBS 16:30 AMP

IF YOU KEEP TELLING YOUR SON SOMETHING'S WRONG WITH HIM, SOONER OR LATER HE'LL BELIEVE IT. FOLLOW EVERY, "THAT'S WRONG" BY SAYING WHAT'S RIGHT.

While a man was vacationing in the Bahamas, he was sightseeing one afternoon when he noticed a crowd gathered at the end of a pier. He went closer to investigate the commotion and discovered that a young man was making last-minute preparations for a solo journey around the world in a home-made boat. Without exception, everyone on the pier was trying to talk him out of his voyage, telling him everything they thought could go wrong with the trip: "The sun will broil you!" "You don't have enough food." "That boat won't make it through a storm." "You'll never make it."

In spite of all these dire warnings, the opti-mistic and ambitious young sailor pushed away from the dock. As he sailed away, the observer ran to the end of the pier and with both arms waving wildly, he shouted: "BON VOYAGE! You're really something! We're with you. We're proud of you! Hurry back!"

After the sailboat was out of earshot, he turned and found the crowd staring at him in dis-belief. "Do you really believe that?" one man asked. The tourist replied, "I don't know. But if he gets into trouble, I hope he remembers my words, not yours."

Say to your child, "Go for it!" And then pray they make it.

And I myself also am persuaded of you, my brethren, that ye also are full of goodness, filled with all knowledge . . .

ROMANS 15:14

YOU CAN'T DO MUCH
ABOUT YOUR
ANCESTORS BUT
YOU CAN INFLUENCE
YOUR
DESCENDANTS
ENORMOUSLY.

Consider the lives of two men. One of them, Max Jukes, lived in New York. He did not believe in Christ or give Christian training to his children. He refused to take his children to church even when they asked to attend. He had 1,026 descendants—300 of whom were sent to prison for an average term of thirteen years. Some 190 were public prostitutes and 680 were admitted alcoholics. His family members cost the state in excess of $420,000—thus far—and they have made no known positive contributions to society.

Jonathan Edwards lived in the same state and at the same time. He loved the Lord and saw that his children were in church every Sunday. He served the Lord to the best of his ability. Of his 929 descendants, 430 were ministers, 86 became university professors, 13 became university presidents, 75 wrote positive books, 7 were elected to the U. S. Congress, and one served as vice-president of the United States. His family never cost the state one cent but contributed immeasurably to the common good.

Ask yourself: if my family tree began with me, what fruit might it bear two hundred years from now?

... but as for me and my house, we will serve the Lord.

JOSHUA 24:15

EVERY DAD IS THE FAMILY ROLE MODEL, WHETHER HE WANTS THE JOB OR NOT.

Pitching great Orel Hershiser is often regarded as a role model for young people today. But who was his primary role model? In his book *Out of the Blue*, Hershiser describes his role model as a man who was very competitive, yet generous and a gentleman. "In everything he does," says Hershiser, "he wants to win. . . . Sometimes he would compete only with himself. I saw that side of him even in how he cleaned the garage. He took care of every detail and put everything in its place."

He always commended and rewarded those who did a good job. A perfectionist, he often demanded that a job be done repeatedly, but even so, he gave a pat on the back in encouragement. He didn't mind pain and he didn't mind work. And he had a grand habit of asking "why?" When others might say in the face of a weather prediction of rain, "There goes our golf date tomorrow," he would say instead, "Why? Does the weatherman have to be right? We don't know what tomorrow will be like. The storm may pass through. Let's plan on playing and see if it works out." He was a stubborn optimistic, with a never-give-up attitude.

Who was this superlative role model? His dad!

. . . in order to offer ourselves as a model for you, that you might follow our example.

2 THESSALONIANS 3:9 NAS

CHILDREN ARE LIKE CLOCKS; THEY MUST BE ALLOWED TO RUN.

For a number of years, "flea circuses" were quite popular. Today, few people have seen a flea circus, much less know how fleas come to be trained.

When fleas are first put into a jar, they jump wildly. Since fleas are incredible jumpers, a lid must be put on even a large jar in order to keep the fleas contained. Still, they continue to jump, hitting their heads on the lid again and again. Over time, however, the fleas no longer jump as high as they did initially. Most of them jump to a height that is just a fraction of an inch from beneath the lid.

At this point, a flea trainer can remove the lid from the jar. The fleas will continue to jump, but now, they no longer jump out of the jar. The reason is simple. They have conditioned themselves to jump only so high. Once conditioned to jump to that height, that's all they can do! They will never again regain their ability to jump higher.

Have you "capped" your child in some way today? Have you built a ceiling so low for your child that he is forever hitting his head? Remove that lid quickly! Otherwise, you may forever stunt his concept of his own potential!

Fathers, . . . do not be hard on them (children) or harass them; lest they become discouraged.

COLOSSIANS 3:21 AMP

THE CHILD THAT NEVER LEARNED TO OBEY HIS PARENTS IN THE HOME I WILL NOT OBEY GOD OR MAN OUT OF THE HOME.

Susanne Wesley, mother of John and Charles Wesley was a God-fearing mother of seventeen children. Many of her principles for child training appear in John Wesley's journal, such as:

"When turned a year old (and some before), they were taught to fear the rod, and to cry softly; by which means they escaped abundance of correction they might otherwise have had; and that most odious noise of the crying of children was rarely heard in the house; but the family usually lived in as much quietness as if there had not been a child among them.

"In order to form the minds of children, the first thing to be done is to conquer the will, and bring them to an obedient temper. To inform the understanding is a work of time, and must with children proceed by slow degrees as they are able to bear it; but subjecting the will is a thing which must be done at once; and the sooner the better. For by neglecting timely correction they will contract a stubbornness and obstinacy which is hardly ever after conquered.

"Self-will is the root of all sin and misery, so whatever cherishes this in children insures their after-wretchedness; whatever checks and mortifies it promotes their future happiness."

Children, obey your parents in the Lord; for this is right.

EPHESIANS 6:1

BY PROFESSION I AM A SOLDIER AND TAKE PRIDE IN THAT FACT, BUT I AM PROUDER TO BE A FATHER.

A Navy fighter pilot, Lt. Cmdr. John E. Bartocci was stationed aboard the aircraft carrier Bon Homme Richard during the Vietnam War. His letters home during 1976 reveal his great love for his family:

31 Jan. Three years of shore duty were wonderful. The children's characters have really taken shape. I know them so much better now, and that makes leaving so much more difficult.

6 May. After the pressures of this air war, 1 know what a treasure the serenity of the family is. I long to feel the children's arms around me, to play the role of the lion with his cubs. Tears come to my eyes when I think how I want to be with my children, playing with them, explaining things to them, trying to give them some of myself.

12 June. I'm looking at the beautiful pictures you sent me of the children. I see such *hope* in their eyes. I want so much to hold them in my arms . . . to be there to influence my children, to bring out their good qualities. What greater success can a father ask?

Six weeks later, Bartocci was killed when his aircraft crashed while returning from a night mission.

Hug your children today. Tell them how much you love them. Learn to treasure and make the most out of every day you have with your children.

I have great confidence in you; I take great pride in you . . .

2 CORINTHIANS 7:4 NIV

THE STRONGEST
EVIDENCE OF
LOVE IS
SACRIFICE.

Andrew Wyermann's favorite Christmas memory took place when he was seven years old. He recalls, "Early Christmas Eve, my mother took my brother and me out for a treat. It was her way to get us out of our fifth-floor apartment in the Bronx while my father prepared for the evening festivity. As we climbed the stairs back to the apartment, the shrill sound of a whistle filled the hallway. What was that, and where did it come from? Our pace quickened and a second burst of the whistle could be heard. We dashed into the apartment. There was my father playing engineer with the biggest Lionel train ever made. It was so magnificent, so unexpected, so wonderful!

"Some fifty years later, I still have the train set and cherish it . . . The train is a warm reminder of the greater gift my parents gave me. This gift has nothing to do with any material advantages, or even with any piece of sage advice. Unconditional love was their gift. I never doubted their care for me, and from such grace sprang my own capacity to truth. It was years later that I fully understood the gift my parents gave me had its source in God's gift of the Child to us all. The sound of the whistle and the song of the angels have become one and the same."

For God so loved the world, that he gave his only begotten Son, that whosoever believeth in him should not perish, but have everlasting life.

JOHN 3:16

GOVERN A
FAMILY AS YOU
WOULD COOK A
SMALL FISH—
VERY GENTLY.

A delaida Blanton tells of a "five minute rule" that she had in her home when she was a child. "What it meant," she explains, "was that we were all to be ready for school five minutes before we actually had to leave."

"We were a large family and that extra five minutes was prayer time for Mother and us children. The place was wherever Mother happened to be when we were all ready to leave. Sometimes it was the kitchen, other times the living room or bedroom, or even out on the porch. But we all kneeled while Mother asked a blessing on each of us individually and thanked the Lord for His provision for us. Often all of our names were spoken and some special blessing asked for each.

"If a neighborhood child dropped in to walk to school with us (and neighbors often did), they were included in our prayer circle, too.

"When the prayer was finished, there came a kiss for each, and we were off.

"Those were *Five Important Minutes* to each of us."

Aren't there five minutes you can find today for a gentle, and godly, timeout with your child?

And the servant of the Lord must not strive; but be gentle unto all men.

2 TIMOTHY 2:24

WORDS HAVE AN
AWESOME IMPACT.
THE IMPRESSIONS
MADE BY A
FATHER'S VOICE
CAN SET IN MOTION
AN ENTIRE TREND
OF LIFE.

Arthur's father only had to give an order once and one of his commandments was, "There's to be no hanging around. If he ain't workin' or someplace special, a man is supposed to be home." Arthur and his brother Johnnie were taught to work hard and love the family. Arthur's dad also said, "You gain by helping others." To match deed to word, he would take his sons with him to deliver old clothes, food, and wood to families in need. He also said, "You don't get nowhere by making enemies." Arthur never forgot.

As an internationally renowned tennis player, Arthur Ashe arose at five o'clock on summer days, hit 500 balls, ate breakfast, and then hit 500 more. He was known for his drive on the court, and his gentleman's demeanor off the court. He built a strong family. His wife, Jeanne, and his daughter Camera, were the light of his life. He started the Safe Passage Foundation to help poor youngsters learn tennis, golf, and fencing, and also improve their scholastic skills. And all his adult life, he fought to bring blacks and whites closer together.

What Arthur Ashe, Sr., said, he did. And so, too, Arthur Ashe, Jr.

Death and life are in the power of the tongue: and they that love it shall eat the fruit thereof

PROVERBS 18:21

LIKE FATHER,
LIKE SON:
EVERY GOOD
TREE MAKETH
GOOD FRUITS.

A little boy was given a globe of the world as a gift. He especially liked the fact that it had a light in it. The little boy put it in a secure spot in his room, and not only looked at it often during the day, but used it as a night light in his room at bedtime.

One night his parents were debating a point of geography when one of them remembered the globe in their son's room. Dad went to get the globe for reference, quietly tiptoeing into his child's semi-dark room and unplugging it. Just as he was almost out the door, his son called to him in a sleepy voice, "Daddy, what are you doing with my world?"

What an important question for any father to ask himself! What is it that you are doing with your child's world today? How are you managing it? What are you planting in it? How are you developing it? . . . But equally important, how are you dealing with your own world? Your child isn't likely to reflect any greater spiritual, moral, or ethical values than those you hold. He isn't likely to learn what you don't teach or encourage. He isn't likely to be much different than you! Because, to a great extent . . . you are his world. What you do with your own life is the foundation on which his world is built.

Even so every good tree bringeth forth good fruit . . . .

MATTHEW 7:17

AN INFALLIBLE
WAY TO MAKE
YOUR CHILD
MISERABLE IS
TO SATISFY ALL
HIS DEMANDS.

The sheriff's office in a Texas city once published and distributed a list of rules titled "How to Raise a Juvenile Delinquent in Your Own Family." Among the advice given were these admonitions:

Begin with infancy to give the child everything he wants.

This will insure his believing that the world owes him a living.

Pick up everything he leaves lying around.

This will teach him he can always throw off responsibility on others.

Take his part against neighbors, teachers, and policemen. Teach him that they are all prejudiced against your child and that he is a "free spirit" and never wrong.

This will instill in him that he is to have no regard for any person who ever attempts to correct him or limit his behavior.

Finally, prepare yourself for a life of grief.

You're going to have it.

A child who never hears the word no has a limited understanding of the word yes.

The rod and reproof give wisdom: but a child left to himself bringeth . . . shame.

PROVERBS 29:15

PERFORMANCE UNDER STRESS IS ONE TEST OF EFFECTIVE LEADERSHIP. IT MAY ALSO BE THE PROOF OF ACCOMPLISHMENT WHEN IT COMES TO EVALUATING THE QUALITY OF A FATHER.

F ew doubt the bravery and military skill of General Robert E. Lee. As commander of the Army of Northern Virginia, he was known for shrewdness, fast thinking, an instinct for the counterpunch. He had a keen ability to learn from mistakes and to improvise under the pressure of necessity. Military students still study the way in which he took command and set a course with such mastery that every battle he fought became part of a single campaign.

What many don't know, however, is that Lee had no real taste for war. He much preferred to be at home, romping, playing, and joking with his children, all of whom adored him. The greatest pressure he faced in life was not leading troops, but in being away from his family. On the day before Christmas 1846, he tenderly wrote: "I hope good Santa Claus will fill my Rob's stocking to-night: that Mildred's, Agnes's, and Anna's may break down with good things . . . but if he only leaves for you one half of what I wish, you will want for nothing."

The demands of work may keep you from your family physically, but never let the pressures of work keep you from holding your children in your heart, and telling them they are there.

Cast thy burden upon the Lord, and he shall sustain thee: he shall never suffer the righteous to be moved.

PSALM 55:22

THE MAN WHO
FEARS NO
TRUTHS HAS
NOTHING TO
FEAR FROM
LIES.

I n his November 11, 1942, report on the war to the British House of Commons, Winston Churchill referred to "the soft underbelly of the Axis." On the surface, Hitler's regime seemed anything but soft. The powerful blitzkrieg of Nazi troops, the bravado and pageantry of the Third Reich seemed solidly powerful. What the British prime minister perceived, however, was the hidden side of the German dictator: his lack of character, his insecurity, his racially biased fears. He saw the moral darkness of his soul and predicted that when that darkness was exposed, it would create a black hole into which all of the Nazi claims would be sucked into oblivion.

Mark Twain used a similar word picture when he said, "Everyone is a moon, and has a dark side which he never shows to anybody."

When you face up to your own darkness of sin, you can either embrace it and pursue it—which leads to condemnation—or you can repent of sin and turn from it, trusting God to forgive you and flood your dark soul with light. In so doing, you ultimately find that you have no risk of exposure, because there's nothing to expose! You can't be truly embarrassed, because there's nothing you are desperate to hide.

. . . may your love and your truth always protect me.

PSALM 40:11 NIV

MEN WILL SPEND
THEIR HEALTH
GETTING WEALTH;
THEN GLADLY PAY
ALL THEY HAVE
EARNED TO GET
HEALTH BACK.

Many people think that having money would solve all their problems. Consider the words of five of the wealthiest Americans in history:

John D. Rockefeller said, "I have made many millions, but they have brought me no happiness. I would barter them all for the days I sat on an office stool in Cleveland and counted myself rich on three dollars a week." Broken in health despite his Christian beliefs, Rockefeller employed an armed guard in his latter years to ensure his personal safety.

W. H. Vanderbilt said, "The care of 200 million dollars is too great a load for any brain or back to bear. It is enough to kill anyone. There is no pleasure in it."

Wealthy businessman John Jacob Astor was a martyr to dyspepsia and melancholy who once said, "I am the most miserable man on earth."

Automobile king Henry Ford said, "Work is the only pleasure . . . I was happier when doing a mechanic's job." Multimillionaire Andrew Carnegie once noted, "Millionaires seldom smile."

Money cannot satisfy the deep needs of the human heart. Learn to value your health because all the money in the world cannot buy it.

People who want to get rich fall into temptation and a trap and into many foolish and harmful desires that plunge men into ruin and destruction.

1 TIMOTHY 6:9 NIV

MANY A MAN SPANKS HIS CHILDREN FOR THINGS HOW OWN FATHER SHOULD HAVE SPANKED HIM FOR.

Near the top of one of the highest peaks in the Rocky Mountain range—more than 10,000 feet above sea level—are two natural springs. They are so close together and level in height, that it would not take a great deal of effort to divert one streamlet toward the other. Yet . . . if you follow the course of one of these streams, you will find that it travels easterly, and after traversing plateaus and valleys, receiving water from countless tributaries, it becomes part of the great Mississippi River and empties into the Gulf of Mexico.

If you follow the water from the other fountain, you will find that it descends gradually in a westerly direction, again combining with other tributaries until it becomes part of the Columbia River, which empties into the Pacific Ocean.

The terminal points of the two streams are more than five thousand miles apart, separated by one of the highest ranges of mountains in the world. And yet in their onset, the two streams are close neighbors. Very little effort would be required to make the easterly stream run west, or the westerly stream run east.

If you want to impact the course of a life . . . start at birth!

Withhold not correction from the child: for if thou beatest him with the rod, he shall not die. Thou shalt beat him with the rod, and shalt deliver his soul from hell.

PROVERBS 23:13-14

THE FIRST DUTY
OF LOVE IS TO
LISTEN.

Author and pastor's wife Colleen Townsend Evans has written, "Silence need not be awkward or embarrassing, for to be with one you love, without the need for words, is a beautiful and satisfying form of communication.

"I remember times when our children used to come running to me, all of them chattering at once about the events of their day—and it was wonderful to have them share their feelings with me. But there were also the times when they came to me wanting only to be held, to have me stroke their heads and caress them into sleep. And so it is, sometimes, with us and with God our Father."

Don't force your child to talk to you. Give him the respect and "space" to remain silent. Sometimes children need to work out their own ideas and opinions in quiet before voicing them. On the other hand, when he does talk, take time to listen intently, carefully, and kindly. In so doing, your child will know that he can talk to you whenever he wants or needs to, and you can rest assured that his silence is not rooted in suspicion or fear of you.

The language of silence is a language.

Wherefore, my beloved brethren, let every man be swift to hear . . .

JAMES 1:19

HE THAT WILL HAVE
HIS SON HAVE
RESPECT FOR HIM
AND HIS ORDERS,
MUST HIMSELF
HAVE A GREAT
REVERENCE FOR HIS
SON.

The parent who truly cares is a parent who will be available to give applause. Children take great delight in performing if they know their parents are in the audience, and are present not solely for their own pleasure or enjoyment. This is even true for preschoolers.

A group of nursery school children was once overheard having this conversation:

> Child #1: "My daddy is a doctor and he makes lots of money and we have a swimming pool."
>
> Child #2: "My daddy is a lawyer and he flies to Washington and talks to the president."
>
> Child #3: "My daddy owns a company and we have our own airplane."
>
> Child #4—to the envy of all the other children: "My daddy is here!"

Children regard the public presence of their parents as a visible symbol of caring and connection that is far more important to them than any amount of material support. Be there for your child today. He'll remember your *presence* far more than your *presents*.

Be devoted to one another in brotherly love; give preference to one another in honor.

ROMANS 12:10 NAS

NO PERSON WAS
EVER HONORED FOR
WHAT HE RECEIVED.
HONOR HAS BEEN
THE REWARD FOR
WHAT HE GAVE.

He received two degrees, including a master of science degree. He was elected a fellow of the Society for the Encouragement of Arts, Manufactures, and Commerce in London and won the Spingarn Medal. He received a $100,000-a-year job offer from Thomas A. Edison. He received visits from Presidents Calvin Coolidge and Franklin Roosevelt, and an invitation from Joseph Stalin to superintend plantations in southern Russia. Yet for all he received, George Washington Carver is best known for what he gave.

He dedicated his life to making Tuskegee Institute an instrument of ministry to the needs of rural blacks—teaching them how to become skilled farmers and useful citizens. He taught better ways of tilling the soil, the importance of a balanced diet, and called upon black farmers to grow a variety of crops—including peanuts, sweet potatoes, and cowpeas—instead of only cotton. He led the way toward the development of more than 300 derivative food and industrial products from peanuts, and more than 100 from sweet potatoes.

In the end, your resume of accomplishments will mean little. Your gifts to others will count most!

. . . the righteous giveth and spareth not.

PROVERBS 21:26

RESPONSIBILITY IS THE THING PEOPLE DREAD MOST OF ALL. YET IT IS THE ONE THING IN THE WORLD THAT DEVELOPS US, GIVES US MANHOOD . . . FIBRE.

One responsibility that we all have is the responsibility to do our best, which is to strive toward perfection. Consider the implications of people giving only a 99.9 percent performance in these areas:

· Two million documents would be lost by the Internal Revenue Service this year.

· Twelve babies would be given to the wrong parents each day.

· Some 291 pacemaker operations would be performed incorrectly.

· Twenty thousand incorrect prescriptions would be written.

· Shoe manufacturers would ship out 114,500 mismatched pairs of shoes.

None of us will ever achieve perfection in all areas of our lives. But neither do any of us have an excuse for failing to try to do a one-hundred-per-cent job. As the owner of the Ritz-Carlton Hotels said after his enterprise received the prestigious Malcolm Baldrige National Quality Award, "Quality is a race with no finish line."

"Giving it your best" means "going for the top."

Blessed is that servant, whom his lord when he cometh shall find so doing.

LUKE 12:43

. . . WE CAN EITHER GRACE OUR CHILDREN, OR DAMN THEM WITH UNREQUITED WOUNDS WHICH NEVER SEEM TO HEAL . . . MEN, AS FATHERS YOU HAVE SUCH POWER!

A man once told this poignant story about his own conversion experience: "My father was the senior elder in our church for many years. When I was a boy, eleven years of age, an evangelist held a series of meetings in our church. One night he asked every Christian to come forward and also asked those who desired to confess Christ to come with them. My father, of course, went up, and, as I felt the call of God, I followed after him.

"Just as he reached the front he turned around, and seeing me, said, Johnnie, you go back; you are too young.' I obeyed him, as I had been taught to do, and at thirty-three I came again, but I did not know what I was coming for as clearly at thirty-three as I did at eleven.

"The church lost twenty-two years of service, while I lost twenty-two years of growth because my own father, an officer in the church, had said, 'Go back.'"

If you err at all, err on the side of your child knowing God, of his being old enough to experience God, and of his being mature enough to respond to God's offer of love and forgiveness.

Death and life are in the power of the tongue: and they that love it shall eat the fruit thereof.

PROVERBS 18:21

PERHAPS ONCE IN A HUNDRED YEARS A PERSON MAY BE MINED BY EXCESSIVE PRAISE, BUT SURELY ONCE EVERY MINUTE SOMEONE DIES INSIDE FOR A LACK OF IT.

Joan Benoit, the 1984 gold medalist in the first women's Olympic marathon, writes in her book, *Running Tide*:

"The neighborhood beach association hired a lifeguard for the summer. He was also a Red Cross certified instructor in water safety; every summer he gave out certificates to kids who passed the Red Cross swimming tests.

"While I did not sink like a piece of lead in salt-water, I was no great swimmer either. Every summer I was I determined to show that lifeguard I could pass his tests, and every summer I failed. Every year the lifeguard watched me try once, then as much as said I should forget it. I think he believed I was hopeless. But I refused to be dis-couraged . . . His attitude made me so mad I vowed I would never give up. I kept working at it for the next three summers . . . Finally, when I was thirteen, I earned my Junior Lifesaving and Water Safety card.

"My feelings were hurt, not so much by the lifeguard as by my own limitations. I looked up to him because he was a one of the best athletes my town had produced; I wanted to impress him and never did. He had no idea I was knocking myself out for a few kind words."

Let no corrupt communication proceed out of your mouth, but that which is good to the use of edifying, that it may minister grace unto the hearers.

EPHESIANS 4:29

TO BECOME A
FATHER IS NOT
HARD, TO BE A
FATHER IS,
HOWEVER.

Your child makes you a father. As a father, you have the privilege not only of making your child, but of molding and preparing your child for all eternity. No greater job description could ever be given to you!

Donald Grey Barnhouse has written a brief essay on "Father and Son," in which he says:

If a man begets a son, in consequence of that act, he is always, the father of that son. There have been men who have been fathers of sons who have never been fathers to their sons. But many a man who begets a child, gives himself to that child. He is with the mother in the training of the child. The boy is with the father in his free moments. The father enters into the boy's studies; he participates in the boy's games. He makes the boy's hobbies his own hobbies. No question of the boy is beyond the patience of the father. He explains things to the child in great detail whenever the child shows interest in an answer. He trains the boy, leads him on, truly educates him. It can be said in the highest degree that this man is not only father of the boy, he is father to the boy.

Get all advice you can and be wise the rest of your life.

PROVERBS 19:20 TLB

OPPORTUNITIES FOR MEANINGFUL COMMUNICATION BETWEEN FATHERS AND SONS MUST BE CREATED. AND IT'S WORK TO ACHIEVE.

Most communication researchers and theorists contend that the first step in effective communication is "gaining attention." In order to establish lines of communication with your children, you first must "attend" to them—really see them, really hear them, really listen to them, really feel what they feel.

The Hebrew word for attend has several meanings. Two of them paint vivid descriptions about the listening process:

> • *a sharpened ear.* Such ears are like those of an animal listening to an unusual sound. Imagine a dog's ears being "picked up" or "perked up" to listen. That's the picture of a sharpened ear! As a father, you are challenged to tune in to your children, to listen to them with a heightened awareness.
>
> • *a bent ear.* This is the ear that is "cocked" in a certain direction—the ear positioned so that it hears fully and clearly, without distortion. As a father, put away anything that might distract you from listening to your child with your whole heart, mind, and spirit. Bend your ear in your child's direction.

This type of active listening takes effort. It can be far more draining than talking. But it is also the foremost key to communicating with your child!

To every thing there is a season, . . . a time to keep silence, and a time to speak.

ECCLESIASTES 3:1,7B

Shortly after President Franklin D. Roosevelt began his law practice as a young man in New York, he was retained to handle a very difficult and involved civil case. The opposing lawyer was a man of great experience, and had a reputation for very effective closing statements to juries. Indeed, he completely outshone young Roosevelt in his arguments to the jury. He made one fatal mistake, however. His closing argument took several hours!

As the older and more experienced lawyer spoke on and on in his thunderous voice, Roosevelt noticed that the jury didn't seem to be paying much attention to him. So, playing a hunch when his turn came to speak, he rose and said: "Gentlemen, you have heard the evidence. You also have listened to my distinguished colleague, a brilliant orator. If you believe him, and disbelieve the evidence, you will have to decide in his favor. That's all I have to say."

The jury was out for only five minutes before it brought in a verdict in favor of Roosevelt's client.

Those who speak at length tend to lose their audience.

Those who listen at length tend to gain a friend.

Seest thou a man that is hasty in his words? them is more hope of a fool than of him.

PROVERBS 29:20

DON'T BE A LION
IN YOUR OWN
HOUSE.

A tyrannical husband once demanded that his wife conform to a rigid set of standards of his own choosing. She was to do certain things for him as a wife, keep house a certain way, dress a certain way, treat her children a certain way, speak and act in public a certain way. She tried to please her husband but over time, she came to hate his list of rules and regulations. Not surprisingly, she soon grew to hate him. Then, one day the man died—an act of God's mercy, as far as the wife was concerned.

Some time later, she fell in love with another man and married him. To her surprise, she found that she and her new husband seemed to be on a perpetual honeymoon. Joyfully, she devoted herself to his good welfare. One day while cleaning out some boxes in the attic, she came across one of the sheets of do's and don'ts her first husband had written for her to follow. To her amazement, she realized she was doing for her second husband all the things her first husband had demanded, even though her new husband had never once suggested them. She had been giving as an expression of love, not out of obedience to a demand.

Love and serve your wife . . . and you're likely to receive all the tender-loving care you can receive!

Not lording it over those entrusted to you .
.
1 PETER 5:3 NIV

TRAIN YOUR CHILD IN THE WAY IN WHICH YOU KNOW YOU SHOULD HAVE GONE YOURSELF.

M ost of us know of the Great Depression that occurred during the 1930s, but few know about the financial depression in the first half of the 1800s. Governments—from city to state to national—went into financial panic. Pennsylvania, one of the wealthier states at the time, repudiated its debts . . . in effect declaring itself insolvent. Illinois, then a fairly poor state, felt that with such a move made by its wealthy neighbor, it might be justified in doing likewise.

When Stephen Douglas heard of the proposal for repudiation, he opposed it strongly. Although he was very ill, he insisted that he be carried to the state legislature on a stretcher. Lying on his back he made this historic resolution: "That Illinois be honest." The motion touched the hearts of every member of the state house and the resolution was adopted with enthusiasm. The action by Illinois kept the practice of repudiation from spreading among the states. And many historians credit this move as a key reason Illinois is one of the most prosperous states today.

Taking the right road sometimes means taking the unpopular road with the highest toll. Teach your child that there is no substitute, however, for the rewards at the end of such a journey.

I will instruct thee and teach thee in the way which thou shalt go: I will guide thee with mine eye.

PSALM 32:8

Willie had good cause to judge his father. His dad and mom had been teenage sweethearts and had married at age eighteen. But then his father abandoned his mother when she became pregnant and Willie didn't meet his father until nineteen years later.

He said, "I was eager but nervous to meet my father. I didn't know what to expect. What I discovered was a kind, loving, sincere person, who actually cared for me. He and I talked for a long time. I began to understand his reasons for running away. I learned a lot about life and about myself from that conversation. I never held a grudge against my father.

. . . My father had his reasons for leaving. It wouldn't be fair to compare his life with mine. It would be like comparing baseball and football. I simply accepted my father as he was. I didn't offer judgment on what he had done, and I eventually grew to love him for what he was."

Yes, Willie Stargell—an All-Star outfielder who played twenty years for the Pittsburgh Pirates—had good reason to criticize the father he never knew as a child . . . but he didn't.

You may think you have good cause to criticize another . . . but is it ever a good *enough* cause?

Do not judge lest you be judged. For in the way you judge, you will be judged; and by your standard of measure, it will be measured to you.

MATTHEW 7:1-2 NAS

GOD SENDS NO ONE AWAY EXCEPT THOSE WHO ARE FULL OF THEMSELVES.

In the last century, an American tourist heard that a renowned Polish rabbi, Hofetz Chaim, lived in the area where he was traveling. A great admirer of Rabbi Chaim, he asked if he might be able to visit him at his home. Word came back from the rabbi that he was welcome to stop by at any time.

The excited young tourist arrived at the rabbi's home and was invited to take off his knapsack and come inside. He entered the doorway to find only a simple one-room lodging. It was filled with books. The furnishings were limited to a table, a lamp, and a cot.

The tourist asked in amazement, "Rabbi, where is the rest of your furniture?" Hofetz Chaim replied, "Where is yours?"

The puzzled American replied, glancing out the door at his knapsack, "My furniture? But I'm only a visitor here." The rabbi responded, "So am I."

Very often it is when we empty ourselves not only of our pride, but of the possessions we pride ourselves in, that we truly can find those things which will last for all eternity It is impossible to grasp hold of Heaven and earth with the same outstretched hand.

for God resisteth the proud, and giveth grace to the humble.

1 PETER 5:5

THERE IS NO MORE VITAL CALLING OR VOCATION THAN FATHERING.

At the close of the sixteenth century, King Henry IV of France once was interrupted in his royal chamber by the Spanish ambassador. The envoy stood in astonishment at the sight he saw before him. There was the King of France on the floor, playing the part of horse while his young son rode atop his back. Although the diplomat was speechless at the sight, the king was matter of fact. "You are a father, too, Señor Ambassador," he said, "so we will finish our ride."

While a significant part of fathering is to provide a role model for a child to "look up to," an important aspect of fathering requires a man to get down on his child's level . . . indeed, to enter their world for play and exploration, and while there, to provide comfort, solace, and assistance. The challenge is often not to be the "big man" around the house, but to engage in the life of the "little ones." As Henry Ward Beecher once noted, "Men cannot be developed perfectly who have not been compelled to bring children up to manhood. You might as well say that a tree is a perfect tree without leaf or blossom, as to say that a man is a man who has gone through life without experiencing the influences that come from bending down, and giving one's self up to those who are helpless and little."

I press toward the mark for the prize of the high calling of God in Christ Jesus.

PHILIPPIANS 3:14

THE MEASURE OF A MAN IS NOT WHAT HE DOES ON SUNDAY, BUT RATHER WHO HE IS MONDAY THROUGH SATURDAY.

n *Growing Wise in Family Life*, Charles R. Swindoll has written: "You know what's helped us in the Swindoll home? To think of where we live as a training place, not a show-place. The home is a laboratory where experiments are tried out. It is a place where life makes up its mind. The home is a place where a child is free to think, to talk, to try out ideas. In a scene like that, God fits very comfortably into the entire conversation. And at any place where His name is inserted, it fits . . .

"Isn't that comfortable? Ready for a shocker? It's supposed to be comfortable! Christianity is designed for everyday living. Society has made it a 'Sunday religion.' But true-to-life Christianity is designed for Tuesday afternoon just as beautifully as Saturday morning or Sunday evening Thank goodness, you don't have to dress up for it. It fits after a meal as well as before bedtime."

Christianity is meant to be a spill-over religion—to fill up a person to *overflowing*. Our faith is meant to spill over into every day of the week, every action we take, every word we speak, and every relationship we have. It's meant to spill over from our hearts to the hearts of others.

. . . that you may live worthy of the Lord and may please him in every way: bearing fruit in every good work . . .

COLOSSIANS 1:10 NIV

THE WORLD IS
BLESSED MOST
BY MEN WHO DO
THINGS, AND
NOT BY THOSE
WHO MERELY
TALK ABOUT
THEM.

An old man once showed up at the back door of the house rented by a couple of college students. As they cracked open the door, they saw his eyes were glassy and his face unshaven. He bid them a good morning and then offered them some of the produce he was carrying in an old wicker basket. Although the produce was far from appealing, the students made a purchase, mostly to alleviate their pity and fear.

The visits became more regular. The students began to realize the glaze on his eyes was the result of cataracts, not alcohol. They became accustomed to his shuffling by, sometimes wearing mismatched shoes. He frequently punctuated his conversations by pulling out a harmonica to play Gospel tunes.

On one visit he said, "God is so good! I came out of my shack this morning and found a bag full of shoes and clothing on my porch." The students rejoiced with him, "We're happy for you!" Then he added, "You know what's even more wonderful? Just yesterday I met some people who could really use 'em."

No matter how little you may have or how little you know, you still have something you can do for both yourself and for others. As the old adage advises: talk only about the faith you live.

But be ye doers of the word, and not hearers only, deceiving your own selves.

JAMES 1:22

AUTHORITY WITHOUT WISDOM IS LIKE A HEAVY AX WITHOUT AN EDGE, FITTER TO BRUISE THAN POLISH.

A number of years ago, an urgent and unusual invitation went out to a man to come quickly to a military academy. The students there had mutinied and the administrators hoped this particular man might help resolve the situation. The students were protesting against virtually everything: their classes, study hours, drill. The principal handed the mediator a large number of telegrams that had come from the parents of the boys involved. As he read through them, he felt as if he had been given a profile of the types of families from which the boys had come.

One father wired his son, "I expect you to obey." One said, "If you are expelled from school, you needn't come home." Another said, "I'll send you to an insane asylum if you are sent home." Yet another said, "I'll cut you off without a shilling if you disgrace the family."

In the final telegram, however, the mediator found the best message of the day, one from which he drew great hope. The message simply said, "Steady, my boy, steady! Father." "At last," noted the mediator, "here is a man who believes in his son."

There may very well be no greater influence upon a child than to have a father's respect, and to be treated in his or her teenage years as an adult.

. . . the authority the Lord gave me for building you up, not for tearing you down.

1 CORINTHIANS 13:10 NIV

DAD, WHEN YOU COME HOME AT NIGHT WITH ONLY SHATTERED PIECES OF YOUR DREAMS, YOUR LITTLE ONE CAN MEN THEM LIKE NEW WITH TWO MAGIC WORDS— "HI, DAD!"

Perhaps the most famous story told by Jesus is that of "The Prodigal Son" (Luke 15:11-24). The story is that of a young man who requests—and receives—his inheritance while his father is still alive. He takes his new wealth and squanders it, wasting it all in "riotous living." Penniless, he finds himself in a land of famine and ends up feeding swine and eating some of the husks meant for them just to keep his stomach full. No position could have been lower for a young Jewish man!

At that point the boy decides to return home, thinking only to request a position as a servant in his father's house. While he is still some distance from home, his father sees him, rises quickly, and runs to greet him. The story could easily be retitled the parable of "The Happy Father." The father not only kisses his son, but brings out the best robe and puts it on him. He places a ring on his finger and shoes on his feet, fully restoring him to sonship in the family. And then he orders a party in his son's honor.

No person can sadden or gladden the heart of a father like his son. You may know that feeling in your own life as a dad. But . . . does *your* father know it? Does your spiritual father? Does your Heavenly Father?

For we have great joy and consolation in thy love . . .

PHILEMON 7

UNCONDITIONAL LOVE IS LOVING A CHILD NO MATTER WHAT . . . WE EXPECT HIM TO BE, AND MOST DIFFICULT, NO IS MATTER HOW HE ACTS.

A man visited his sister, the director of patient services for the children's unit of a large hospital, and as she gave him a tour through the unit, he heard the cries of a baby echoing through the halls. Finally, the man and his sister came to the child's room. He saw a one-year-old little boy covered with terrible bruises, scratches, and scars from head to toe.

The man assumed that the child must have been involved in a terrible accident. Then he looked closely at the little boy's legs. Written in ink all over them were obscenities. His sister explained that the child was a victim of parental abuse. His internal injuries were so severe that he couldn't keep down food. The scars on the bottom of the baby's feet were the result of cigarette burns.

The woman leaned over the baby's crib and carefully and tenderly lifted up the child and held him close to herself. At first the child screamed all the more, as if he expected to be hurt by human touch. But as she held the child securely, the baby relaxed in her arms and stopped crying. In spite of his wounds and hurts, he soaked up her tenderness like a sponge.

Hold your child close today and let him feel your heartbeat.

But show me unfailing kindness like that of the Lord as long as I live . . .

1 SAMUEL 20:14 NIV

THE VALUE OF
MARRIAGE IS NOT
THAT ADULTS
PRODUCE CHILDREN
BUT THAT CHILDREN
PRODUCE ADULTS.

M any people have thrilled to the voice of the operatic great Beverly Sills. Few know, however, that her natural daughter was born deaf and that she has a stepdaughter who is also severely handicapped.

She writes in her autobiography, *Bubbles*:

"I was now only thirty-four, but a very mature thirty-four. In a strange way my children had brought me an inner peace. The first question I had when I learned of their tragedies was self-pitying 'Why me?' Then gradually it changed to a much more important 'Why them?' Despite their handicaps they were showing enormous strength in continuing to live as normal and constructive lives as possible. How could Peter and I show any less strength?"

Oscar Wilde once wrote: "In this world there are only two tragedies. One is not getting what one wants, and the other is getting it." A third tragedy may be added: the tragedy of not being able to go forward after tragedy has occurred. When a tragedy strikes, our first tendency is to place blame on someone else. It is only when we are willing to accept our part of a tragedy that we truly make progress. It is from that position that we can ask God's forgiveness, and then forgive ourselves and move forward in our lives.

When I was a child, I spake as a child, I understood as a child, I thought as a child: but when I became a man, I put away childish things.

1 CORINTHIANS 13:11

THE BEST WAY TO
TEACH CHARACTER
IS TO HAVE IT
AROUND THE
HOUSE.

On the day before bass season opened, Jimmy and his father were fishing early in the evening on a New England lake. After using worms to catch perch and sunfish, Jimmy decided to practice casting with a small silver lure. No sooner had his lure hit the water than his pole doubled over. Jimmy knew right away that he had something huge on the line. By the time he reeled in the fish, a giant moon had risen over the lake. In the moonlight, Jimmy saw the biggest fish he had ever seen . . . but it was a bass.

Jimmy's dad lit a match to look at his watch:

10 PM, two hours before bass season opened. "You'll have to put it back, son," he said. Jimmy protested, "There'll never be another fish as big as this one!" He looked and saw no other fishermen or boats. Still, he knew by the tone of his father's voice that there would be no discussion. He carefully worked the hook from the lip of the bass and lowered it back into the water.

Jimmy was right. He takes his own children to that lake now and in the past thirty-four years, he never has seen a bass that big. But he readily admits that any time he faces a question of ethics, he sees that fish again and has to smile! A decision to do right always lives fresh and sweet in the memory.

A righteous man who walks in his integrity—How blessed are his sons after him.

PROVERBS 20:7 NAS

THE MAN WHO
WINS MAY HAVE
BEEN COUNTED
OUT SEVERAL
TIMES, BUT HE
DIDN'T HEAR
THE REFEREE.

After Dwight Eisenhower won the Republican nomination for President from Robert Taft in a reporter asked Taft about his goals. He replied, "My great goal was to become President of the United States in 1953."

The reporter smirked and said, "Well, you didn't make it, did you?"

Taft responded, "No, but I became senator from Ohio!"

Imagine a target of the type used for playing darts. The bull's eye is usually marked for one hundred points. Concentric rings are labeled 80, 60, 40, 20. Bull's-eye scores are rare; players often hit lesser-valued rings. But nearly every dart player will tell you that if he doesn't aim for the bull's eye, he scores lower than he would other-wise. And the person who doesn't aim and throw at all, scores zero!

A person once said, "I would rather attempt to do something great for God and fail, than to do nothing and succeed." Another has said, "Shoot for the moon. Even if you don't make it, you'll land among the stars."

For though a righteous man falls seven
times, he rises again . . .

PROVERBS 24:16 NIV

KEEP COMPANY
WITH GOOD MEN
AND GOOD MEN
YOU WILL
IMITATE.

Our friends and associations during our youth are like a prophecy of our future character and destiny.

Voltaire's agnosticism has been traced by some to the *Abbe de Chateuneuf*, who, although a priest, sowed the seeds of deism in Voltaire. One can only imagine that with a different environment in his youth, Voltaire might have been just as powerful a voice for the faith as he became for unbelief.

The English philosopher John Locke, on the other hand, had Lord Somers as a friend and counselor during his youth. Somers has been described as "one of those divine men who like a chapel in a palace, remains unprofaned, while all the rest is tyranny, corruption, and folly." He left his mark on Locke.

John Wesley, while at Oxford, determined to have no friends other than those who could help him in the life of faith he was trying to lead.

Help your child choose his or her friends wisely. And on your child's behalf, choose wise teachers, mentors, and counselors for your child. The choice of your child's influencers may be among the greatest choices you ever make as a father.

Iron sharpeneth iron; so a man sharpeneth the countenance of his friend.

PROVERBS 27:17

THE GREAT MAN
IS HE WHO DOES
NOT LOSE HIS
CHILD'S HEART.

A little boy named Jay Rial loved the sound of the train whistle that brought the circus to town. He loved the circus band, the clowns, the animals. He loved the performers and the very tent itself. He loved the smell of peanuts, the roar of the lions, and the beautiful ladies who rode the beautiful horses. Once he was allowed to stand in the middle of the sawdust-covered ring when they were preparing the tent. It was a great moment for him! Little Jay Rial vowed, "If I ever get to be a big man, I'm going to take just as many children to the circus with me as I can." He called it his circus dream.

It was a dream he remembered. As an adult, Jay Rial went into the circus business as an "advance man." Each year when the circus came to the biggest city on its tour, Jay Rial arranged for every child in every hospital and orphanage—as well as any child who was crippled or not as fortunate as other children—to come to the circus free. When more children showed up than the tent could hold, Jay Rial didn't turn them away. He arranged for *another* circus party!

Jay Rial's childhood dream came true. And in the process, he also made dreams come true for countless children.

And he shall turn the heart of the fathers to the children, and the heart of the children to their fathers . . .

MALACHI 4:6

AN OUNCE OF LOVING ROLE MODELING IS WORTH A POUND OF PARENTAL PRESSURE.

A boy lost his left arm at the shoulder when he was only seven years old. Until he was twelve, he cried himself to sleep every night. He found it impossible to see the amputation as ever having any good outcome. Gradually, however, he began to conquer his handicap. By tucking a long-handled hoe under his armpit, he soon learned to hoe as many rows as his brothers.

Later in life, he sold life insurance, and was very successful at it. He learned to play handball and at one time, held the national championship in that sport. He also became adept at golf, hunting, and fishing.

One day he learned of a thirteen-year-old boy who had gone through a similar amputation. The boy had no will to live and his condition was worsening. The man took his scrapbook and went to the hospital to see the boy. Nothing was said about the arm, but as the boy looked at the various newspaper clippings he finally asked, "Is this you?" The man removed his shirt and showed the boy his armless shoulder. The boy sighed deeply and soon fell asleep. Three days later he was on the mend and soon after, he left the hospital.

You are the first and foremost role model your child will have. What you "show" to your child will be vastly more influential than what you "tell" your child.

In everything set them an example by doing what is good.

TITUS 2:7 NIV

EVERY CHILD COMES WITH THE MESSAGE THAT GOD IS NOT YET DISCOURAGED OF MAN.

A little shepherd boy was watching his sheep one Sunday morning. As he heard the bells ringing the faithful to church, and watched the people walking to church along the lane next to the pasture, he began to think a that he, too, would like to communicate with God. *But what can I say?* he thought. He had never learned a prayer. So, on bended knee, he began to recite the alphabet—A, B, C, D, and so on to Z, repeating his "prayer" several times.

A man passing by heard the boy's voice and looking through the bushes, he saw the young man kneeling with folded hands, closed eyes, saying, "J, K, L, M . . ." He interrupted the boy, asking, "What are you doing, my little friend?" The boy replied, "I was praying, sir." The man seemed surprised and said, "But why are you reciting the alphabet?"

The boy explained, "I don't know any prayers, sir. But I want God to take care of me and help me to care for the sheep. So, I thought if I said all I knew, He could put the letters together into words and spell all that I want and should say." The man smiled and said, "Bless your heart. You're right. God will!" and went on to church, knowing he had already heard the finest sermon he could possibly hear that day.

What is man, that thou art mindful of him? and the son of man, that thou visitest him? For thou hast made him a little lower than the angels, and hast crowned him with glory and honour.

PSALM 8:4-5

MY FATHER IS
THE STANDARD
BY WHICH ALL
SUBSEQUENT
MEN IN MY LIFE
HAVE BEEN
JUDGED.

Two million dollars to the *Cite Universitaire* in France, the restoration of Rheims Cathedral, the repair of palaces at Versailles and Fontainebleau, $500,000 for the Shakespeare Memorial Theatre at Stratford-on-Avon, $4 million for Acadia National Park, $500,000 for Jewish farm development in Russia, 54 acres for a New York city park, $3.5 million to the New York Public Library . . . the list goes on and on! Most of the gifts are credited to John D. Rockefeller, but it was his son who made the decisions about how to distribute the money accumulated by his father. Shortly before his father's 94th birthday, J. D. Rockefeller, Jr., wrote to his father:

"I have tried to do what I thought you would have me do . . . I have endeavored to use wisely and unselfishly the means that you have so unselfishly placed at my disposal . . . In all these years of effort and striving, your own life and example have ever been to me the most powerful and stimulating influence. What you have done for humanity and business on a vast scale has impressed me profoundly. To have been a silent partner with you in carrying out these great constructive purposes and benefactions has been the supreme delight of my life."

. . . leaving us an example, that ye should follow his steps.

1 PETER 2:21

SOME PARENTS BRING UP THEIR CHILDREN ON THUNDER AND LIGHTNING, BUT THUNDER AND LIGHTNING NEVER YET MADE ANYTHING GROW.

A family once planned a month's vacation to the West Coast. At the last minute, the father was unable to go because of work responsibilities. Mom insisted she was capable of driving and she and the children went ahead with their trip. Dad helped plan their route and arranged where they would stop each night.

As it turned out, Dad was able to complete his work within two weeks. He decided to surprise the family, so he flew to a West Coast city without calling them. Then he took a taxi out of the city and asked to be let off along the highway on which, according to his travel plan, the family should be driving later that day. When he saw the family car, he stuck out his thumb as a hitchhiker. As Mom and the children drove past, they did a double-take. One of the children exclaimed, "Mom, wasn't that Dad!" The car came to a screeching stop, and the family enjoyed a joyful reunion.

When a reporter later asked the man why he did such a crazy thing, he said, "After I die, I want my kids to be able to say, 'Dad sure was fun, wasn't he?'"

Laughter and fun times are like gentle rain on your child's personality. Not only do they cause your child to flourish, but they enable the fertilizer of guidance and discipline to soak in.

. . . you should practice tenderhearted mercy and kindness to others . . . Most of all, let love guide your life . . .

COLOSSIANS 3:12,14 TLB

MY DAD AND I HUNTED AND FISHED TOGETHER. HOW COULD I GET ANGRY AT THIS MAN WHO TOOK THE TIME TO BE WITH ME?

D uring war games, Private Glenn Sollie and Private Andrew Bearshield of the Fifteenth Infantry were ordered to make their way to a bridge and stand guard there until they were relieved.

The two were faithful soldiers. They went to the bridge and guarded it . . . and guarded it. They stuck to their job for three days and nights, with neither food nor blankets. They eventually were found rather than "relieved." The two privates had been guarding the wrong bridge! They had lost their way and taken their battle stations at a bridge seven miles away from the one they were to guard. One might suppose they were reprimanded for making such a mistake. On the contrary, they were given military honors for guarding their position with such faithfulness!

Very often our parents make mistakes in life. They can make "wrong turns" or follow what turn out to be foolish pursuits. But rather than criticize them or blame them for their errors, we can choose to focus on what they did right! In turning our attention to their positive qualities and deeds—however meager they may be—we usually find we have no difficulty giving them "honor."

Honor thy father . . .

EXODUS 20:12

UNLESS A
FATHER
ACCEPTS HIS
FAULTS, HE
WILL MOST
CERTAINLY
DOUBT HIS
VIRTUES.

A father lost his temper one morning in one of those "irritating situations" that tend to happen in life. He unleashed his frustration and anger on his son, who happened to be the closest "target." Later in the day, while he and his son were fishing, he became convicted about what he had said and done. He began, "Son, I was a little impatient this morning."

"Uh huh," the son grunted, reeling in his line and preparing to cast again. The father continued, "Uh . . . I realize I was a little hard to be around."

Again, "Uh huh" was the only response his son made. The father continued, "I . . . I want you to know that, uh . . . I feel bad about it." Then quick to justify himself he added, "But you know, son, there are times that I'm like that." The boy merely said, "Uh huh."

A few seconds passed, and then the boy added, "You know, Dad. God uses you to teach all of us in the family patience."

Our families have a way of "nailing us" with their honesty, but rather than feeling hammered, take what they say as good advice. Nobody else can help you grow into the nature of Christ Jesus as much as your family members!

. . . he hath made us accepted in the beloved.

EPHESIAN 1:6

WHAT WAS SILENT
IN THE FATHER
SPEAKS IN THE SON,
AND OFTEN I HAVE
FOUND THE SON THE
UNVEILED SECRET
OF THE FATHER.

While a grown man was awaiting surgery in a hospital he began talking with his father. "I sure hope I can be home by Father's Day," he said. The two recalled various Father's Day celebrations they had shared through the years and then the son said wistfully, "I still feel awful that when I was ten years old, I didn't give you either a card or a gift."

The father replied, "Son, I remember the Saturday before that Father's Day. I saw you in a store although you didn't see me. I watched as you picked up several cigars and stuffed them in your pocket. I knew you had no money and I suspected you were about to steal those cigars as a present for me. I felt extremely sad to think you would leave the store without paying for them. But almost as soon as you tucked the cigars in your pocket, you pulled them out and put them back in the box on the shelf.

"When you stayed out playing all the next day because you had no present to give me, you probably thought I was hurt. You were wrong. When you put those cigars back and decided not to break the law, you gave me the best Father's Day present I ever received."

And he did that which was right in the sight of the Lord . . . as Joash his father did.

2 KINGS 14:3

Charles Lindbergh, although a celebrity who achieved international fame, remained an enigma to many people. Few could understand why he did not seek to capitalize more on his historic flight across the Atlantic in 1927. Commercializing the flight seemed to be the last thing Lindbergh wanted to do.

One person estimated that Lindbergh could have made five million dollars in one week if he had accepted the hundreds of offers he received to sign testimonials, write books, or go into the movies. William Randolph Hearst alone offered him half a million dollars to star in a film about aviation. He was offered a vaudeville contract with a one-million-dollar guarantee. A movie company made him a million-dollar offer and another movie company upped its offer to five million. All were turned down. Others sent money to Lindbergh as gifts. All of it was returned.

An associate of Lindbergh summed up Lindbergh's perspective on these many ways he might have added fortune to his fame. He said simply, "Lindbergh won't take money he hasn't earned."

The money one *gains* in life counts for little if it isn't *earned* legally and morally, and if it isn't *spent* in accordance with sound values.

The just man walketh in his integrity.

PROVERBS 20:7

A MAN'S CHILDREN AND HIS GARDEN BOTH REFLECT THE AMOUNT OF WEEDING DONE DURING THE GROWING SEASON.

Pastor Stephen Bly writes in *How to Be a Good Dad*:

"When we first moved to northern Idaho, our front yard consisted of nothing but weeds. Sooner or later, we had to tackle the yard. Mike, at fifteen, seemed a likely prospect to handle the job. But about five minutes after starting, he came back into the house. 'I need some gloves,' he reported . . . he spent twenty minutes looking for gloves. After a brief time back in the yard, he returned again. 'I've got to have some music 'He spent fifteen minutes setting up his portable stereo . . . Ten minutes later I saw him again. 'It's hot out there. I've got to have a drink.' Finally, I thought I heard him chopping. But not for long . . . 'Hey, Dad,' he said, 'you know what we need? . . . If we had one of those electric weed whips . . .'

"'Mike!' I began in my best drill sergeant's voice, 'I don't care if it takes you all day, all week, or all month. You and that hoe are going to chop down every weed. Then you're going to rake them and carry them off. Now, stop stalling.'"

Bly concludes, "I'm sure I sounded insensitive . . . but I did care. I cared enough to know that Mike, like all of us, needed to learn to put in a hard day's work. Caring dads teach good work habits."

He who spares his rod hates his son, but he who loves him disciplines him diligently.

PROVERBS 13:24 NAS

IF IT IS DESIRABLE THAT CHILDREN BE KIND, APPRECIATIVE, AND PLEASANT, THEN THOSE QUALITIES SHOULD BE TAUGHT—NOT HOPED FOR.

A king once decided to honor the greatest of his subjects. Word went throughout the kingdom and various recommendations were immediately forthcoming. A man of wealth and property was singled out. One person was lauded for her healing skills, another for his fair practice of the law. Still another was praised for his honesty in business and yet another for his bravery as a soldier. Each person for the candidate of "greatest" was brought to the palace and presented to the king. He admitted to his counselors that this choice was going to be very difficult.

As the last day before the honor ceremony arrived, the last candidate was finally brought before the king—a white-haired woman whose eyes sparkled with the light of knowledge, love, and understanding.

"Who is this?" the king asked. "What has she accomplished of note?" An aide replied, "You have seen and heard all the other candidates. This woman is their teacher." Those in the court erupted into applause and the king immediately stepped from his throne to honor her.

Virtues do not happen by accident or as a natural part of growth. As with any skill or means of success, they must be taught.

For the commandment is a lamp; and the law is a light; and reproofs of instruction are the way of life.

PROVERBS 6:23

*E*ncounter once published this list of "Ten Things for Which You as a Parent Will Never Be Sorry":

1. For doing your level best even when discouraged.
2. For hearing before judging in family quarrels.
3. For thinking before speaking when emotionally upset.
4. For not harboring unkind thoughts of a tale-bearer.
5. For being generous to an enemy, perhaps the next-door neighbor.
6. For stopping your ears to gossip over the fence.
7. For standing by your principles in dealing with your teenagers.
8. For asking pardon, when in error, even of your child.
9. For being square in business dealings with the newsboy.
10. For accepting the stewardship of "another" child.

Most of us know the ideals of being a good parent. Putting those ideals into practice is what's hard—but also what is most rewarding!

Therefore all things whatsoever ye would that men should do to you, do ye even so to them . . . .

MATTHEW 7:12

TO BE SUCCESSFUL IN THE FAMILY THE FATHER MUST HAVE THE WELFARE OF EACH FAMILY MEMBER AT HEART AND HIS DECISIONS AND PLANS MUST BE BASED UPON WHAT IS BEST FOR THEM.

A twelve-year-old girl named Susan hated sharing a bedroom with her seven-year-old sister. She dreamed of being an only child with a room all her own. Apparently her father seemed to have the same idea. He was attending night school and longed for a room where he could study in quiet, away from his noisy family. He decided to build such a room for himself. Throughout the summer months, he poured the foundation, hammered, sawed, and installed wiring and windows. Although work slowed during the autumn months, the heat was finally connected, the carpet laid, and the built-in bookshelf completed.

On the last day before Christmas vacation, Susan came home from school to find the bedroom she shared with her sister completely rearranged. Angry with her sister for having upset the room, she raced down the hall after her into the new addition to the house. There, her parents greeted her with a shout of "Surprise!" To Susan's amazement, she found that all her possessions had been moved, her clothes hung in the closet, her books placed on the shelves.

"Daddy knew you needed your own room," her mother said, "so he decided you should have this one."

Do nothing from selfishness or empty conceit, but with humility of mind let each of you regard one another as more important than himself.

PHILIPPIANS 2:3 NAS

CHILDREN MISS NOTHING IN SIZING UP THEIR PARENTS. IF YOU ARE ONLY HALF CONVINCED OF YOUR BELIEFS, THEY WILL QUICKLY DISCERN THAT FACT.

Karl, a young Jewish boy in Germany, had a profound sense of admiration for his father. The life of the family centered around the acts of piety and devotion prescribed by their religion. The father was zealous in attending worship and instruction, and demanded the same from his children. When Karl was just a teenager, the family moved. Their new town had no synagogue. To Karl's surprise, his father announced to the family that they were going to abandon their Jewish traditions and join the Lutheran church. He explained that this was necessary to help his business, since the leading citizens of the town were Lutheran.

Karl was both disappointed and confused by this action. His bewilderment gave way to anger and an intense bitterness that remained within him throughout his life. He left Germany and went to England to study. While there, he conceived of a movement that he hoped would change the entire world, and he wrote a manuscript of his ideas. In his book he termed religion as an "opiate for the masses" that could be explained in strictly economic terms. Billions of people eventually came to live under the government system conceived by Karl Marx—it was called communism.

Let us holdfast the profession of our faith without wavering . . .

HEBREWS 10:23

CHILDREN ARE OUR MOST VALUABLE NATURAL RESOURCE.

Martin Luther had a reputation as an excellent father who used just the right way of discipline and love. He believed: "Punish if you must, but let the sugarplum go with the rod." He composed songs for his children, playing his lute while his children sang them. His letters to his children are jewels.

Luther especially had a tender place in his heart for his daughter Magdalena, about whom he said, "God has given no bishop so great a gift in a thousand years as He has given me in her." When she became ill at the age of fourteen, he prayed constantly for her, finally praying, "I love her very much, but, dear God, if it is Thy holy will to take her, I would gladly leave her with Thee." To Lena he said, "Dear, my little daughter, thou wouldst love to remain here with thy father; art thou willing to go to that other Father?" His daughter said, "Yes, dear father, just as God wills." When she died, he wept long and as she was laid in the earth he spoke to her as to a living soul: "You will rise and shine like the stars and the sun."

Most of us think of natural resources and riches as coming from the earth. May none of us have to lay a precious child into the earth to realize that our child has been far more valuable to us than earth's riches.

Children are an heritage of the Lord . . .

PSALM 127:3

A YOUNG
BRANCH TAKES
ON ALL THE
BENDS THAT
ONE GIVES TO IT.

Stan's father was general manager of a road construction company. One day when Stan was about ten years old, he went with his father to the shop. Paving materials were stockpiled there, including a pile of rock. Being a Little League player, Stan felt compelled to throw a few of those rocks while his father went inside the shop. Unfortunately, one of the rocks put a big spiderweb crack in the windshield of his dad's car!

No one was around and Stan's first thought was to blame the crack on the kids from a poor part of town who customarily passed the shop about that time each day. Still, Stan wasn't comfortable with a lie. When his father returned to the car, Stan was there waiting. With tears in his eyes, he told his father what had happened, fully expecting to be punished soundly. His father surprised him, however, by calling the incident an accident. He noted that Stan could have blamed others, and he admired his honesty. And then, he told his son that since he felt it was right for Stan to pay part of the damages, he would be forced to adjust Stan's weekly allowance—which he did—from 25 cents a week up to 50 cents a week so he could pay a quarter a week toward the new windshield!

Train up a child in the way he should go: and when he is old, he will not depart from it.

PROVERBS 26:6

IF THERE BE
ANY TRUER
MEASURE OF A
MAN THAN BY
WHAT HE DOES,
IT MUST BE BY
WHAT HE GIVES.

At a church meeting a very wealthy man rose to give a testimony. "I'm a million-aire," he said, not at all humbly. "I attribute it all to the rich blessings of God in my life. I came from a wonderful family. He gave me abundant intelligence and good business sense. I worked hard. On the night after I received my first pay-check, I went to a church meeting. The speaker was a missionary who told about his work. I gave everything I had to God. I believe that God blessed that decision, and that is why I am a rich man today."

After smiling broadly at the congregation, he sat down. After a few seconds of silence in the church, a tiny elderly woman sitting in the pew behind him leaned forward and said, "I dare you to do it again."

Pride in self is the very antithesis of a good heart. As a missionary discovered when he attempted to translate the word "pride" for a tribe noted for its mutuality of sharing, pride can be a difficult concept to define. Yet, it is one universally recog-nized. The missionary finally attached an air pump to a bicycle tire and, while pointing first to one head and then to another, began to pump hard until the tire inflated to several times its size . . . and burst. Everyone in the village nodded in understanding!

. . . it is more blessed to give than to receive.

ACTS 20:35

MEN FOR THE SAKE OF GETTING A LIVING FORGET TO LIVE.

At a Rotary meeting in Illinois a number of years ago, Gypsy Smith gave a stirring speech to the leading business and professional men of the city. As he prepared to close his remarks, he lifted his well-worn Bible high above his head and then asked the men in attendance, "How many of you men can recall a saintly mother and a godly father who loved this Book, read it, lived it, and seeped it into you?"

Nearly every man in the room, with moist eyes and sober expression, raised a hand.

Then quietly and deftly, Gypsy made his final statement. "With all your influence today, how many of you are so living that your children will remember you for your faithfulness to this same Book?"

It was a tense moment. The point had sunk deep into the hearts of those in attendance, bringing conviction and a silence in which one might hear a pin drop. Not a hand was raised.

If you were asked these two questions today, how would you answer them?

In all of our "earning" a living, may we never forget the joy of the life we have already been given as a gift and a godly heritage.

It is vain for you to rise up early, to take rest late, to eat the bread of (anxious) toil—for He gives (blessings) to His beloved in sleep.

PSALM 127:2 AMP

IF A MAN CANNOT BE A CHRISTIAN IN THE PLACE WHERE HE IS, HE CANNOT BE A CHRISTIAN ANYWHERE.

Fifteen-year-old Heidi doubled over with stomach pains while backpacking. After being rushed to the hospital and undergoing surgery to stop her internal bleeding, Heidi seemed to recover quickly. Then tests revealed an adrenal tumor. Heidi underwent more surgery, followed by extensive radiation. She asked her father, "Why me, Dad?" Her father answered, "Honey, the Book of Matthew says, 'Ye are the light of the world . . . Let your light so shine before men, that they may see your good works, and glorify your Father which is in heaven.' I know you have accepted Jesus as your personal Saviour and have become one of His lights, sweetheart."

Two years later, Paul watched his "light" Heidi receive her high-school diploma, and then the cancer struck again, this time in her lungs. As Paul embraced his daughter, he could say only, "Honey, all we can do is call on the Lord for His strength." Another surgery followed. And the following Christmas Paul again witnessed joy as his "light" Heidi married. The following April, Heidi died as a result of brain cancer.

How hard it is for a father to be a Christian when his daughter is suffering and dying! Paul saw Heidi as one of God's "lights," but surely he was also a light to her in her greatest hours of need.

Let your light so shine before men, that they may see your good works, and glorify your Father which is in heaven.

MATTHEW 5:16

YOU CANNOT LIVE A PERFECT DAY WITHOUT DOING SOMETHING FOR SOMEONE WHO WILL NEVER BE ABLE TO REPAY YOU.

When Frank arrived at the Pearly Gates, he very quickly found himself standing face to face with an impressive angelic being holding a clipboard. The angel told Frank he needed to get some "entry data"—name, address, a few other particulars. As part of the form completion, the angel said, "Frank, it would help if you could identify one experience from your life on earth in which you did a purely unselfish, kind deed."

Frank thought for a few seconds and then said, "Well, I think I have something that qualifies. One day as I was walking, I came upon a little old lady who was being beaten mercilessly by a rough motorcycle gang member. He was smacking her around so I stepped right up and pushed over his motorcycle—but only to distract him. Then I kicked him real hard in the shins and shouted for the old lady to run for help. Then I hauled off and put my fist right into the guy's stomach. I think the old lady made it to safety."

"Wow," the angel replied, "that is very impressive." Then, with pen poised on his clipboard, he asked, "When did this happen?" Frank looked at his watch and replied, "Oh, two or three minutes ago."

Make today a perfect day by doing something for someone who can never repay you!

And do not forget to do good and share with others, for with such sacrifices God is pleased.

HEBREWS 13:16 NIV

FROM GOOD
PARENTS COME
A GOOD SON.

During his tenure as president of Princeton University, Woodrow Wilson was once asked to speak to a parents' group. He said, in part: "I get many letters from you parents about your children. You want to know why we people up here in Princeton can't make more out of them and do more for them. Let me tell you the reason we can't. It may shock you just a little, but I am not trying to be rude. The reason is that they are your sons, reared in your homes, blood of your blood, bone of your bone. They have absorbed the ideals of your homes. You have formed and fashioned them. They are your sons. In those malleable, moldable years of their lives you have forever left your imprint upon them."

While most parents hope their children will enjoy a higher standard of living than they themselves have experienced, what many parents fail to realize is that a child will rarely exhibit a higher standard of morality, ambition, and godliness than that which his parents displayed. We can never expect a teacher, pastor, mentor, counselor, friend, or Sunday school teacher to impart to our children that which only we as parents can give and do. You are the main "star" in your child's life. All others are supporting actors.

A good tree cannot bear bad fruit . . .

MATTHEW 7:18 NIV

AMONG ALL THE ABUSES OF THE WORLD . . . THERE IS NONE WORSE THAN A NEGLIGENT FATHER.

After several months in a therapy group, Stuart decided to visit his twenty-year-old son at college. He asked the boy what it had been like to have him as a father. "Well, Dad," he said, "I don't want to hurt your feelings . . . but you were never there."

"What do you mean?" Stuart asked. "I was there every evening. I never went anywhere!" The boy said, "I know, Dad, but it was like there was nothing to you. You never got mad. If you were ever sad, I never knew it. You never seemed happy . . . I didn't know who you were. You were like a stranger to me . . . most of the time I felt like I didn't have a father."

In relating this back to his therapy group, Stuart broke down and cried for the first time in more than forty years. "Can you believe it?" he asked. "I was there . . . and he felt I was invisible."

Eventually Stuart got past his dismay and went through a real emotional growth surge. He joined an outdoor club and took his son white-water rafting and deep-sea fishing. One night he told the group, "I'm so angry. So much of my life has been wasted. And what I really regret is that I've hurt my son—not because I ever did anything mean, but because there was so little inside of me for him to see."

It is never too late. Let your child see "inside" of you.

> But you have neglected the more important matter of the law—justice, mercy, and faithfulness
>
> MATTHEW 23:23C NIV

CHILDREN NEED
LOVE,
ESPECIALLY
WHEN THEY DO
NOT DESERVE
IT.

A shepherd once had a sheep that ate from his hand and followed him everywhere. When he was asked to explain the close relationship, the shepherd smiled and replied that this particular sheep had once been the most wayward in his flock.

In its first year of life, the sheep had wandered away numerous times, costing the shepherd many long hours of searching. Finally, the shepherd broke the lamb's leg. He then bound the leg in a splint and carried the sheep with him to the hills. There, he fed it by hand and brought it water to drink. Day by day he took care of the lamb until it had fully recovered.

After that, the sheep never went astray again. In fact, it followed the shepherd more closely than a dog might follow its master.

Expressions of love to a child very often involve discipline coupled with closeness of caring. When a child errs and strays from what is right, it is then that a parent must show love in extraordinary ways—coupling any disciplinary action with tenderness and closeness. The purpose of such discipline must always be like that of the Great Shepherd, who "restoreth" our souls.

Therefore be imitators of God, as beloved children; and walk in love, just as Christ also loved you, and gave Himself up for us, an offering and a sacrifice to God as a fragrant aroma.

EPHESIANS 5:1-2 NAS

PRAISE YOUR
CHILDREN
OPENLY,
REPROVE THEM
SECRETLY.

Young Teddy once listened as his father told, at great length and in great detail, about a time in the past when Teddy showed great wisdom and poise under fire. The child kept tugging at his dad's pants leg all the while he was talking. The father, annoyed, finally leaned over to see what his son wanted. "Dad," the child whispered loudly, "That wasn't me. It was Billy!" Embarrassed before his friend, the father took Teddy by the arm and marched him to the wood-shed.

All the way there, Teddy kept saying, "Dad, Dad." The father, at wit's end, stopped and said, "Now what? I suppose you're going to tell me that Billy is the one who openly ridiculed me in front of my friend?"

"No," said the boy. "I'm hoping that when you see your friend tomorrow you can brag about how you didn't punish me even when you wanted to."

Whether praising or correcting your child, make sure you are telling the truth! Open and truthful praise before others builds up your child . . . but lies or false flattery creates false self-esteem. Secret correction spares your child humiliation, and retains your child's dignity and self-respect. But reproof that is unfounded or rooted in falsehood can cause great damage, even if spoken behind closed doors.

> Correct thy son, and he shall give thee rest; yea, he shall give delight unto thy soul.
>
> PROVERBS 29:17

EVERY MAN IS ENTHUSIASTIC AT TIMES. ONE MAN HAS ENTHUSIASM FOR THIRTY MINUTES, ANOTHER HAS IT FOR THIRTY DAYS—BUT IT IS THE MAN THAT HAS IT FOR THIRTY YEARS WHO MAKES A SUCCESS IN LIFE.

Three ditch diggers were on the job one day. An o' observer watched as one man leaned on his shovel and began to brag about how he was going to be a foreman in the ditch-digging company some day. The second man then stopped to lean on his shovel as he began to complain about the long hours, the hard work, and the low pay. The third man just kept digging.

Years went by. The observer came across a ditch-digging crew in the same area and asked about the three men he had seen years before. To his surprise, one of the men stopped digging, leaned on his shovel, and said, "Why, I was one of those men." He was still leaning on his shovel!

"And your friends?" the observer asked.

"Oh," said the man, "ol' Sam was always complaining about this and that, and one day he just up and said he was injured. Don't know what happened . . . but he's been on disability ever since."

"And the third man?"

The ditch digger replied, "Why he owns the whole company now."

. . . let us run with perseverance the race marked out for us.

HEBREWS 12:1 NIV

MEASURE WEALTH
NOT BY THE THINGS
YOU HAVE, BUT BY
THE THINGS YOU
HAVE FOR WHICH
YOU WOULD NOT
TAKE MONEY.

During the Depression, many families could scarcely afford the bare essentials, much less purchase presents at Christmas. "But, I'll tell you what we can do," said the father to his six-year-old son, Pete. "We can use our imaginations and make pictures of the presents we would like to give each other."

For the next few days, each member of the family worked secretly, but with joy. On Christmas morning, huddled around a scraggly tree decorated with pitifully few decorations, the family gathered to exchange the presents they had created. And what gifts they were! Daddy got a shiny black limousine and a red motor boat. Mom received a diamond bracelet and new hat. Little Pete had fun opening his gifts, a drawing of a swimming pool and pictures of toys cut from magazines.

Then it was Pete's turn to give his present to his parents. With great delight, he handed them a brightly colored crayon drawing of three people—man, woman, and little boy. They had their arms around one another and under the picture was one word: US. Even though other Christmases were far more prosperous for this family, no Christmas in the family's memory stands out as more precious!

. . .for a man's life consisteth not in the abundance of the things which he possesseth.

LUKE 12:15

IT TAKES TIME TO BE A GOOD FATHER. IT TAKES EFFORT—TRYING, FAILING, AND TRYING AGAIN.

While at the park one day, a woman sat down next to a man on a bench near a playground. "That's my son over there," she said, pointing to a little boy in a red sweater who was gliding down the slide. "He's a fine looking boy," the man said. "That's my son on the swing in the blue sweater." Then, looking at his watch, he called to his son, "What do you say we go, Sam?"

Sam pleaded, "Just five more minutes, Dad. Please? Just five more minutes." The man nodded and Sam continued to swing to his heart's content.

Minutes passed and the father stood and called again to his son, "Time to go now?" Again Sam pleaded, "Five more minutes, Dad. Just five more minutes." The man smiled and said, "Okay."

"My, you certainly are a patient father," the woman responded.

The man smiled and then said, "My older son Tommy was killed by a drunk driver last year while he was riding his bike near here. I never spent much time with Tommy and now I'd give any-thing for just five more minutes with him. I've vowed not to make the same mistake with Sam. He thinks *he* has five more minutes to swing. The truth is, I get five more minutes to watch him play."

And let us not get tired of doing what is right, for after a while we will reap a harvest of blessing if we don't get discouraged and give up.

GALATIANS 6:9 TLB

CHILDREN DESPERATELY NEED TO KNOW—TO HEAR IN WAYS THEY UNDERSTAND AND REMEMBER—THAT THEY'RE LOVED AND VALUED BY MOM AND DAD.

Lee Iacocca, former president of Ford Motor Company and former CEO of Chrysler Corporation, writes in his book, *Straight Talk*:

"My parents spent a lot of time with me, and I wanted my kids to be treated with as much love and care as I got. Well, that's a noble objective . . . but to translate it into daily life, you really have to work at it.

"I spent all my weekends with the kids and all my vacations. Kathi was on the swim team for seven years, and I never missed a meet. Then there were tennis matches . . . and piano recitals. I made all of them too. I was always afraid that if I missed one, Kathi might finish first or finish last and I would . . . not be there to congratulate—or console—her.

"The same with Lia . . . Once I picked up Lia at Brownie camp. She was six years old and came running out to the car in her new khaki uniform with an orange bandana around her neck and a little beanie on her head. She had just made it into the Potawatomi Tribe. She had hoped to join the Nava-joes, as she called them, but she was turned down. Still, she was excited, and so was I. Funny thing, I missed an important meeting that day, but for the life of me I have no recollection of what it was."

. . . let us stop just saying we love people; let us really love them, and show it by our actions.

1 JOHN 3:18 TLB

HAPPINESS IS INWARD, AND NOT OUTWARD; AND SO, IT DOES NOT DEPEND ON WHAT WE HAVE, BUT ON WHAT WE ARE.

An old legend tells of a tribe that was continually at war with other tribes. This violent tribe murdered, raped, and pillaged their neighbors. They appeared to have no morals, love, or compassion. They were extremely greedy and cruel in their pursuit of success.

An alarmed elder of a benevolent tribe called a conference of reasonable people in tribes throughout the region. They met to see what they might do to save these people from themselves. After much discussion, they decided to take the secret of personal success and happiness away from those who abused it and hide it from them. An elder asked, "Where can we put it so they won't find it?" One person suggested it be buried deep in the earth, another on the top of a mountain. Some suggested it be thrown into the ocean. All concluded, however, that the secret of happiness and personal success could be found in any of these places. Finally, an elder made this proposal: "Let's hide the secret within the people themselves. People like this will never think to look for happiness and success there."

To this day, the waning tribe has continued to pursue success and happiness in many places, never guessing they possess it within.

Beware! Don't always be wishing for what you don't have. For real life and real living are not related to how rich we are.

LUKE 12:15 TLB

THE FOOLISH MAN SEEKS HAPPINESS IN THE DISTANCE; THE WISE GROWS IT UNDER HIS FEET.

A number of years ago, an old friend of John Wanamaker's came to Oak Hall to congratulate the famed department store owner on the store's sixtieth anniversary. He asked politely, "How do you keep?"

Wanamaker replied, "Happily busy."

Sixty years of uninterrupted work in one business is no small achievement. Wanamaker started his own business at the age of twenty-three and developed it into an establishment that became known worldwide. At eighty-three, he was still its head, and he was still making ambitious plans for the future.

His old friend asked him a second question, one that required Wanamaker to reflect on just how he had succeeded when so many others in his field had come and gone through the years. Wanamaker replied again: "It is all in the two words with which I answered your first question. Many people are busy because they have to be; I'm busy because I want to be. So I am happily busy."

Rather than work to earn money so you can have the | life you want . . . work at something you love and at which you are skilled, so that your work becomes a reflection of your very life. Success and money will follow, and you will be satisfied and fulfilled.

. . . for I have learned, in whatsoever state I am, therewith to be content.

PHILIPPIANS 4:11

SELF-ESTEEM ISN'T A LESSON YOU TEACH; IT'S A QUALITY YOU NURTURE.

M arvin Allen tells of meeting Hugh Downs while Downs was taping a special on the men's movement. He writes:

"When I asked Hugh about his dad, his face lit up. He said that he remembered sitting in his dad's lap as a little boy, talking with him for long periods of time. His dad would listen to him and nod thoughtfully, making him feel both wise and worthy of his attention. He talked about the many times his father had taken him to the symphony and explained the names and sounds of the various instruments. He told me of visits to museums and how his dad had discussed art history with him in a way that made it seem fascinating, even to a little boy. As we got to Hugh's cabin, he said that his father had not only shared a great deal of information with him, he had communicated an overall enthusiasm for life.

"I could see how the joy of the father lived on in the son. Hugh's openness to new ideas, his compassion, and his wide-ranging interests are a testimony to how rich life can be for those fortunate men whose fathers were skilled in the art of dispensing usable love."

. . . but bring them up in the nurture and admonition of the Lord.

EPHESIANS 6:4

WHEN WE DO
WHAT WE CAN,
GOD WILL DO
WHAT WE
CAN'T.

A young man was running a race and he found himself falling further and further behind his competitors. His friends cheered him on from the sidelines, but seemingly to no avail. Then suddenly his lips began to move with great regularity, his legs picked up speed, and to the amazement and cheers of the entire crowd watching the race, he passed his competitors one by one . . . and won the race!

After he had been given a blue ribbon and received the congratulations of his coach and teammates, he turned to his friends. One of them asked, "We could see your lips moving but we couldn't hear what you were saying. What were you mumbling out there?"

The young man replied, "Oh, I was talking to God. I told Him, 'Lord, You pick 'em up and I'll put 'em down . . . You pick 'em up and I'll put 'em down!"

When we do the things we know to do, live our lives the way we know God's Word commands us, and we are believing to the best of our ability that the Lord will help us, we are then in a position to know with certainty what the Apostle Paul knew: "I can do all things through Christ which strengtheneth me" (Philippians 4:13).

For with God nothing shall be impossible.

LUKE 1:37

SEEK GOD FIRST
AND THE
THINGS YOU
WANT WILL
SEEK YOU.

D r. George W. Truett once was entertained in the home of a wealthy oilman in Texas. After dinner, the man took Truett up to the roof of his home. Pointing to a field of oil derricks, he said, "Dr. Truett, that's all mine. I came to this country twenty-five years ago penniless, and now I own everything as far as you can see in that direction."

He then turned in the opposite direction, and pointing toward waving fields of grain, he again said, "It's all mine. I own everything as far as you can see in that direction."

He next turned toward the east, pointing to a large herd of cattle . . . and then to the west, pointing to a great virgin forest that extended to the horizon . . . and each time he waved his hands and said, "It's all mine. For twenty-five years I have worked hard and saved, and today I own everything you can see in any direction from my house."

The man paused at that point, expecting words of admiration and praise from Truett. Instead, Dr. Truett laid his hand lovingly on his shoulder, pointed upward, and asked, "And my friend, how much do you own in *that* direction?"

But seek ye first the kingdom of God, and righteousness; and all these things shall be added unto you.

MATTHEW 6:33

THE STRENGTH OF A MAN CONSISTS IN FINDING OUT THE WAY GOD IS GOING, AND GOING THAT WAY.

John Woolman, a 23-year-old clerk in a dry-goods shop, was busy adding up the day's receipts when his employer approached him with another man at his side and said, "John, I've sold Nancy to this gentleman. Draw up a bill of sale for her." As Woolman prepared to do so, something seemed to paralyze his arm. He could not write a word. He declared to his employer, a fellow Quaker, "I believe slave-keeping to be a practice inconsistent with the Christian religion."

The incident deeply troubled Woolman and shortly thereafter, he wrote a pamphlet, *Some Considerations on the Keeping of Negroes*, which was printed by Benjamin Franklin in 1754. Although he became a tailor and orchard keeper, Woolman spent part of every year traveling to preach against slavery. He petitioned the Rhode Island legislature to abolish the slave trade. On a personal level, he stopped eating sugar and wearing indigo-dyed clothes produced as the result of slave labor.

Eventually Woolman traveled to England in his crusade and there, his campaign of writing and speaking resulted in Parliament outlawing the slave trade in 1807 and abolishing slavery in all British colonies by 1933. One man—finding out the way God is going—can change history.

. . . I am the light of the world: he that followeth me shall not walk in darkness, but shall have the light of life.

JOHN 8:12

I OWE ALMOST
EVERYTHING TO
MY FATHER.

A proud father looked at the blue ribbon on the paper before him and began to read what his daughter had written: "We [all] called him 'Daddy' when we were young. He was able to make even folding clothes on Saturday fun with tickle fights amidst freshly washed garments strewn all over the living room floor. He would roll and pretend at vulnerability on the carpet and grab each tiny, groping hand that attempted to tweak his ribs. We seldom won, of course. Daddy could mercilessly tickle . . .

"There were serious times as well. He could spank the tears out of any of us, not because the physical pain was so incredible, but because it hurt us to think that we had brought him pain by having earned that spanking.

"High moral values, spiritual priorities, academic excellence—all these have been held out to us as important. My pop has instilled in us kids a sense of trust. He's been available, especially in emergencies. He has done what he thinks best for us, even when we might not agree . . . My dad has a corner on the upper echelons of fatherhood."

What a tribute! One every father might desire . . . and can earn.

Honour thy father . . . as the Lord thy God
hath commanded thee . . .

DEUTERONOMY 5:16

THE MORE A CHILD
BECOMES AWARE OF
A FATHER'S
WILLINGNESS TO
LISTEN, THE MORE A
FATHER WILL BEGIN
TO HEAR.

Best-selling author Leo Buscaglia's father was determined that each of his children would receive an education. He writes, "Papa believed that the greatest sin was to go to bed at night as ignorant as when we awakened." He insisted that each child learn at least one new thing each day. Dinnertime was the forum for sharing new facts and insights. Buscaglia says, "The news we recounted, no matter how insignificant, was never taken lightly. Mama and Papa listened carefully and were ready with some comment, often profound and analytical, always to the point." At the end of the meal, after Papa had lighted his cigar and taken stock of his family, came the question asked solemnly of each child, "Tell me what you learned today." Before the meal was over, the entire family had been enlightened by at least half a dozen facts.

Buscaglia notes, "In retrospect, I realize what a dynamic educational technique Papa was offering us. Without being aware of it, our family was growing together, sharing experiences and participating in one another's education. And by looking at us, listening to us, respecting our input, affirming our value, giving us a sense of dignity, Papa was unquestionably our most influential teacher."

He that hath ears to hear, let him hear.

MATTHEW 11:15

UNTIL YOU MAKE PEACE WITH WHO YOU ARE, YOU'LL NEVER BE CONTENT WITH WHAT YOU HAVE.

Christy Brown was born in Ireland in 1932 and raised in a Dublin slum. Born with a severe form of cerebral palsy, he could not walk, talk, eat, or drink without help. He never went to school.

One day, one of his siblings was on the floor, drawing letters on a piece of paper with crayons. Christy suddenly moved his left foot, managed to pick up and hold the crayon with his toes, and tried to copy the letters. From that day until his death in 1981, he was only able to use his left foot, typing with his little toe. That was enough, how-ever, for him to be able to write his autobiography, *My Left Foot*, which became a major motion pic-ture. He also wrote two works of fiction. It took him fifteen years to type one of them, *Down All the Days*, but his effort resulted in his being hailed "a man of genius" by the *New York Times*.

Christy Brown never moved from the slums. He fell in love and married. He was a man who first learned to accept his limitations . . . and then to rise above them!

Accept who you are and what you have today. And then use *what you have*. You'll likely find it's enough to bring you to a place of fulfillment in life.

But godliness with contentment is great gain.

1 TIMOTHY 6:6

A GENTLEMAN
IS A *GENTLE*
MAN.

The last passenger to come aboard the flight was a man carried on an ambulance litter. Obviously paralyzed from his shoulders down, he was strapped into his seat tightly. Once airborne, the hostesses began to serve the meal. A man noticed that a tray had been set before the paralyzed man, but that it remained untouched. Seeing that the hostesses were all busy serving other passengers, he slipped into a seat next to the man and asked if he might help. The paralyzed man responded, "Thank you. I would be so grateful."

As the man cut the first few bites and placed them in the paralyzed man's mouth, he felt awkward, but at the same time, much needed. Before long, the two were coordinating bites well and they began to converse. The paralyzed man told of his unfortunate accident, his lonesomeness, his joys, his struggles, his faith. They exchanged names. In a strange way, their spirits blended. The helpful man later concluded, "we experienced sacrament"—a truly sacred moment.

How many people are there who have had the Good News about Jesus Christ set before them, yet they are crippled by spiritual and psychological paralysis . . . and there's no one to feed them? It takes a gentle man to feed a person who cannot feed himself.

And the servant of the Lord must not strive; but be gentle unto all men . . .

2 TIMOTHY 2:24

(THE CALLED MAN) SEES HIMSELF AS A STEWARD . . . HE'S OBEDIENT RATHER THAN AMBITIOUS, COMMITTED RATHER THAN COMPETITIVE. FOR HIM, NOTHING IS MORE IMPORTANT THAN PLEASING THE ONE WHO CALLED HIM.

Stewardship is not something a person decides to do after he or she has made a lot of money. Being a steward is part of being a Christian. Stewardship is the requirement that a person take care of his financial affairs as if he was managing the earthly finances of the Lord Himself.

Walt Meloon once had this to say about the relationship between business and God:

"A businessman has no business being in business just to make money. Every businessman automatically is in danger of making money his god. Whenever he makes a decision in favor of his business as opposed to the Lord Jesus Christ, he has made money his god, for the moment, at least. He is favoring mammon, and his priorities are mixed.

"Advice not to mix Christianity and business is heresy of the worst kind. A man's business, whatever it might be, ought to be an integrated and integral part of his Christianity. It either complements or opposes his spiritual stance."

No matter how hard you try you cannot separate what you have from who you are, and who you are is defined ultimately by who you are to Christ Jesus.

. . . because we obey his commands and do what pleases him.

1 JOHN 3:22 NIV

IF I TAKE CARE
OF MY
CHARACTER,
MY REPUTATION
WILL TAKE CARE
OF ITSELF.

The story is told of a king who owned a valuable diamond, one of the rarest and more perfect in the world. One day the diamond fell and a deep scratch marred its face. The king summoned the best diamond experts in the land to correct the blemish, but they all agreed they could not remove the scratch without cutting away a good part of the surface, thus reducing the weight and value of the diamond.

Finally one expert appeared and assured him that he could fix the diamond without reducing its value. His self-confidence was convincing and the king gave the diamond to the man. In a few days, the artisan returned the diamond to the king, who was amazed to find that the ugly scratch was gone, and in its place was etched a beautiful rose. The former scratch had become the stem of an exquisite flower!

An error we make in life may temporarily mar our reputation. But if we stick to what we know is right and continue to attempt to conform our will to that of God, we can trust Him to turn the "scratches" on our souls into part of His signature—a signature of inner character that truly becomes our eternal reputation.

Righteousness guards the man of integrity.

PROVERBS 13:6 NIV

REMEMBER, WHEN YOUR CHILD HAS A TANTRUM, DON'T HAVE ONE OF YOUR OWN.

A little boy had moved with his parents to a house overlooking a deep ravine. One day his mother reprimanded him for disobeying her and he became very angry, stormed out of the house, and ran to the edge of the ravine. There, to give vent to his feelings, he shouted as loud as he could, "I hate you! I hate you!" Almost immediately, a voice came rumbling back at him in an angry, hollow voice, "I hate you! I hate you!" Startled at first, and then terrified, the little boy raced back into the house. Once in the safety of his mother's arms, he told her there was a wicked man in the ravine who hated him and wanted to do him harm.

The wise mother took her son by the hand and led him back to the ravine. In a tender and cheerful voice she called, "I love you! I love you!" A kind, happy voice echoed back the same sweet words, much to the boy's comfort and delight.

The tantrums of our children can easily disturb us, frustrate us, and even anger us. But just as your child has the ability to impact your mood . . . so you have the ability to impact his! By responding with kindness and good cheer, you can usually turn around a child's tantrum, and maintain your own bright outlook on life at the same time.

Cease from anger, and forsake wrath; fret not thyself in any wise to do evil.

PSALM 37:8

CHILDREN ARE NOT SO DIFFERENT FROM KITES . . . CHILDREN WERE CREATED TO FLY, BUT THEY NEED WIND—THE UNDERGIRDING AND STRENGTH THAT COMES FROM UNCONDITIONAL LOVE, ENCOURAGEMENT, AND PRAYER.

When he was just a boy, John's father made a journey with his family across the American continent. It took the family a full year to make their way from coast to coast. As each sunset and sunrise glorified the skies, the Scotsman would take his children out to show them the skies and speak to them about how the cloud formations were surely "the robes of God."

Who can fathom the full impact this trip had on young John? Or how deeply rooted became his reverence for nature on this year-long journey? What we do know is that John Muir became one of America's greatest naturalists. His a love for nature led him to the mountains, the glacial meadows, and eventually to the icebound bays of Alaska. The lovely Muir Woods in northern California are named in his honor.

What are you "showing" to your children today? What "wind" are you putting under their wings? What examples . . . what encouragements . . . what insights are you giving to your child?

As the Helen Reddy song declared so poignantly more than two decades ago: "You are the wind beneath my wings"—so a parent's influence is for each child.

. . . as a father deals with his own children, encouraging, comforting and urging you to live lives worthy of God.

1 THESSALONIANS 2:11-12 NIV

WHEN THESE PARENTING YEARS HAVE PASSED, SOMETHING PRECIOUS WILL HAVE FLICKERED AND GONE OUT OF MY LIFE. THUS, I AM RESOLVED TO ENJOY EVERYDAY THAT REMAINS IN THIS FATHERING ERA.

Howard was a man in tune with the times. So, when his 4-year-old daughter Melinda acquired a fixation for "The Three Little Pigs" and demanded that her father read it to her night after night, Howard took action. He purchased a child's easy-to-use tape recorder and read the story onto tape for her.

The next time Melinda asked for the story to be read, he switched on the recorder. She was fascinated at the novelty of her father's voice reading her favorite book from a "machine." The following night when she asked for "Free Lil' Pigs," Howard went a step further: he showed Melinda how to work the playback on the recorder for herself.

The following evening, when Melinda arrived and pushed the storybook at him, Howard said, "Now, honey, you know how to turn on the recorder." She smiled and said sweetly but insistently, "Yes." Then she added, "But I can't sit on its lap."

Children need both a father's time and an expression of his affection, including hugs and being held close. A "close" relationship is generally rooted in just that—holding a child close to one's heart always, and close to one's side until it's the child's idea to move to the other end of the sofa.

Redeeming the time . . .

EPHESIANS 5:16

HE THAT WILL
HAVE HIS SON
HAVE A RESPECT
FOR HIM AND HIS
ORDERS MUST
HAVE A GREAT
REVERENCE FOR
HIS SON.

One winter day in Rockefeller Center in New York, a man watched the skaters whirling about on the ice. He found himself drawn to one pair: a teenage girl who was receiving instruction from a brilliant skater. She moved around the rink, making a large circle close to the edge of the rink; her instructor skated a smaller circle toward the center of the rink, executing classical figures even as he kept his eye on her every move. It was easy to see that she was not sure of herself. Several times she nearly fell. But each time she began to become unsteady, in a flash he was by her side, his hand on her elbow helping her maintain her balance.

He said to himself, "What a perfect picture of the life to which the Lord Jesus has called us! God has given to many of us the gift of helping those who are younger . . . or who are in need!" How true this is for fathers, especially. A father is called to keep his eye always upon his children, ready to help, but without show. The unsteady one will know he has been helped, and that the touch at the right moment kept him from falling. But the world will scarcely notice. He will know and the Lord will know, and that is sufficient.

Fathers, do not exasperate your children, instead, bring them up in the training and instruction of the Lord.

EPHESIANS 6:4 NIV

10 COMMANDMENTS FOR
EFFECTIVE FATHERS

-1-

**SPEND TIME WITH
YOUR CHILDREN.**

A man once had a job that required extensive travel. After every long trip, his wife and four children would meet him at the door with loving hugs and kisses. After one such joyful homecoming, he was playing with his youngest child and he asked, "What do you want to be when you grow up?" The child responded without hesitation, "A pilot."

"Why a pilot?" the father asked, a bit surprised.

His daughter looked at him and replied, "So I can spend more time with you." Shortly thereafter, the father took a position that required far less travel!

Most people have a "career lifespan" of forty to fifty years. Experts agree that what an average person earns in the last half of their career is nearly double that of the first half. Parents, by comparison, usually have only twenty to twenty-five years of "active parenting." Even so, many people place far greater emphasis on work during the first half of their career life than they do on family, to the detriment of their children and not much career advancement. Consider another approach! Place emphasis on your *family* during the first twenty years of your career, and then devote full energy to your work during the years when you are wiser, more skilled, and able to earn the most!

Making the very most of the time—buying up each opportunity . . .

EPHESIANS 5:16 AMP

10 COMMANDMENTS FOR
EFFECTIVE FATHERS

-2-

LET YOUR CHILDREN
KNOW OFTEN THAT
YOU LOVE THEM
JUST THE WAY THEY
ARE.

"The Hole in the Wall Gang Camp" was designed and built through the vision and efforts of actor Paul Newman and a group of dedicated volunteers. Opened in 1988, the camp is located on three hundred acres of forest in northeastern Connecticut. It was designed to resemble an Old West logging town of the 1890s. The buildings, facilities, and site make possible a wide range of activities: swimming in a heated outdoor pool, boating, canoeing, fishing, horseback riding, nature walks, woodworking, music, theater, arts, crafts, sports, overnight camping. Children from ages seven to seventeen come to the camp during the summer's four, ten-day sessions.

Sounds like any other summer camp? Hardly. What makes this camp unique, apart from the fact that no camper is charged a fee, is that this camp accepts only children who have cancer, leukemia, and other serious blood diseases—children, who, because of their disease, its treatment, or its complications, cannot attend ordinary camps. The facilities are equipped to meet the medical and physical needs of these special children.

If the founders of a summer camp can accept and love children "just the way they are" how much more should we love and accept our own children.

Wherefore, accept one another, just as Christ also accepted us . . .

ROMANS 15:7 NAS

10 COMMANDMENTS FOR
EFFECTIVE FATHERS

-3-

DISCIPLINE YOUR CHILDREN WHEN THEY NEED IT.

A grandfather once found his grandson jumping up and down in his playpen, crying at the top of his voice. When Joey saw his grandfather, he reached up his chubby hands and cried all the louder, "Out, Gamba, out!"

The grandfather naturally reached down to lift Joey out of his predicament, but as he did, Joey's mother said, "No, Joey, you are being punished— so you must stay in your playpen."

The grandfather felt at a loss as to what to do. On the one hand, he knew he must comply with the mother's efforts to discipline her son. On the other hand, Joey's tears and uplifted hands tugged at his heart. Love found a way! If Gamba couldn't take his grandson out of the playpen, he could climb in and join him there!

Discipline, in its finest form, is "directing a child toward a better way." Discipline goes beyond punishment for a deed to the instilling in a child a desire never to repeat the offending deed, and instead, make a better choice of behaviors. The desire to do right is born of love—the love of the parent for the child, and more importantly, the love of the parent shown to the child.

He who spares his rod hates his son, but he who loves him disciplines him diligently.

PROVERBS 13:24 NAS

10 COMMANDMENTS FOR
EFFECTIVE FATHERS

-4-

**PRAY WITH AND FOR
YOUR CHILD
REGULARLY.**

To hear my child at prayer,
What a thrill it is for me!
There's a sweetness in the moment
As he speaks on bended knee.
And yet my heart is smitten
At this touching sight I see,
Has his faith and trust in prayer
Depended much on me?
As I see him fold his tiny hands
And bow his head to pray,
I trust he'll always love the Lord
The way he does today.
Then I hear a voice within me
Speak in solemn words and true,
"How he lives a life of prayer
Depends a lot on you."
And so I kneel next to the bed,
And lay my hand upon him
After he has voiced his prayer,
I add my own petition.
May my son recall one day
That his father daily raised
His voice to thank the Lord
And make sacrifice of praise!

Wherefore also we pray always for you . . .

2 THESSALONIANS 1:11

10 COMMANDMENTS FOR
EFFECTIVE FATHERS

-5-

**ALWAYS BE HONEST
WITH YOUR
CHILDREN.**

When pitcher Dave Dravecky first noticed the lump on his pitching arm, he had it checked out, but nothing seemed amiss. The lump continued to grow, however, and eventually Dravecky had it biopsied. The result came back: a form of cancer called fibrosarcoma. The treatment called for aggressive surgery to cut away a large part of the bone. Physicians held out little hope he would ever pitch again.

Dave and his wife Janice decided to tell their children, Tiffany and Jonathan, what was happening. As they tucked them into bed one night, they gently explained that Daddy was going to be in the hospital for awhile, and that he probably wouldn't be able to play baseball anymore. They waited for the news to sink in, thinking it would devastate them. Tiffany, however, responded by saying, "You mean we won't have to move anymore? I can stay in my same school? We'll be here in Ohio near Grandma and Grandpa all the time?" Jonathan joined in, "Dad, you mean you'll be able to play football with me every day?"

As much as anything else, their reaction helped Dave Dravecky cope with what lay ahead. In his words, they "put it all into perspective." Be honest with your children. They may help you see things in a new light!

A good man is known by his truthfulness;
a false man by deceit and lies.

PROVERBS 12:17 TLB

10 COMMANDMENTS FOR
EFFECTIVE FATHERS

-6-

LOVE YOUR CHILDREN'S MOTHER.

Helmut Thielicke writes in *How the World Began*, "I once knew a very old married couple who radiated a tremendous happiness. The wife especially, who was almost unable to move because of old age and illness and in whose kind old face the joys and sufferings of many years had etched a hundred lines, was filled with such a gratitude for life that I was touched to the quick. Involuntarily, I asked myself what could possibly be the source of this kindly person's radiance. In every other respect they were common people, and their room indicated only the most modest comfort. But suddenly I knew where it all came from, for I saw those two speaking to each other, and their eyes hanging upon each other. All at once it became clear to me that this woman was dearly loved.

"It was not because she was a cheerful and pleasant person that she was loved by her husband all those years. It was the other way around. Because she was so loved she became the person I saw before me."

You cannot expect your children to show greater respect for their mother—or their own spouses someday—than you show to her.

And you husbands, show the same kind of love to your wives as Christ showed to the church when he died for her.

EPHESIANS 5:25 TLB

10 COMMANDMENTS FOR
EFFECTIVE FATHERS

-7-

TAKE TIME TO
LISTEN TO YOUR
CHILDREN.

Jed Harris, the producer of *Our Town* and numerous other plays, became convinced he was losing his rearing. He went to one physician who couldn't find anything wrong. He referred him to a specialist.

The specialist gave Harris a thorough checkup and nothing showed up to indicate a technical problem with Harris' hearing. The doctor finally pulled out a gold watch and asked, "Can you hear this ticking?"

Harris said, "Of course."

The specialist walked to the door of the examining room and held up the watch again. "Now can you hear it?" he asked.

Harris concentrated and said, "Yes, I can hear it clearly." Finally the doctor walked out the door into the next room and called, "Can you hear it now?"

Harris said, "Yes."

The specialist came back into the examining room and announced, "Mr. Harris, there is nothing wrong with your hearing. You just don't listen."

Really *listen* to your children today. You may be amazed at what you learn from them.

Let the wise listen and add to their learning.

PROVERBS 1:5 NIV

10 COMMANDMENTS FOR
EFFECTIVE FATHERS

-8-

ENCOURAGE YOUR
CHILDREN OFTEN.

Author Phyllis Theroux writes about her father, "If there was any one thing that my father did for me when I was growing up it was to give me the promise that ahead of me was dry land—a bright, marsh-less territory, without chuckholes or traps, where one day I would walk easily and as befitting my talents . . .

"Thus it was, when he came upon me one afternoon sobbing out my unsuccesses into a wet pillow, that he sat down on the bed and . . . assured me that my grief was only a temporary setback. Oh, very temporary! Why he couldn't think of any other little girl who was so talented, so predestined to succeed in every department as I was. 'And don't forget,' he added with a smile, 'that we can trace our ancestry right back to Pepin the Stupid!'

"By the time he had finished talking I really did understand that someday I would live among rational beings, and walk with kind, non-vindictive people who, by virtue of their maturity and mine, would take no pleasure in cruelty and would welcome my presence among them . . . There are some people who carry the flint that lights other people's torches. They get them all excited about . . . the 'can-do' potential of one's own being. That was my father's gift to me.

Therefore encourage one another and build each other up . . .

1 THESSALONIANS 5:11 NIV

10 COMMANDMENTS FOR
EFFECTIVE FATHERS

-9-

**CELEBRATE YOUR
CHILDREN'S
ACHIEVEMENTS.**

Political commentator George F. Will has written lovingly about his son: "Jon Frederick Will, the oldest of my four children, recently turned 21, and on his birthday, as he does on every workday, he commuted by subway to his job delivering mail and being useful in other ways at the National Institutes of Health. That my son is striding into a productive manhood with a spring in his step and Baltimore Orioles on his mind could not have been confidently predicted when he was born . . . Jon has Down syndrome. At the instant he was conceived, he lost one of life's lotteries, but he also was lucky: his physical abnormalities do not impede his vitality, and his mental retardation does not interfere with life's essential joys—receiving love, returning it and reading baseball box scores.

"So one must mind one's language when speaking of people like Jon. He does not 'suffer from' Down syndrome. It is an affliction, but he is happy . . . Happiness, in fact, is a talent, for which Jon has a superior aptitude . . . One aspect of Jon's abnormality . . . is that he is gentleness straight through. Jon is an adornment in a world increasingly stained by anger acted out. He was born on his father's birthday, a gift that keeps on giving."

Rejoice with them that do rejoice . . .

ROMANS 12:15

10 COMMANDMENTS FOR
EFFECTIVE FATHERS

-10-

**BE FLEXIBLE WITH
YOUR CHILDREN.**

Stonecutters use an interesting process to engrave granite. They first paint over a slab of polished granite with a thin coating of rubber. The design for the engraving is penciled onto the rubber and then the rubber is cut away, leaving the stone exposed where the design is to appear. Using compressed air, the stonecutter then blows sand against the granite slab. Where the stone is exposed, the sand cuts into the granite and creates the etching. The areas covered with rubber remain unaffected.

Sand can be blown upon the rubber for an hour without making an imprint, even though sand blown against granite for that long would likely bore a hole completely through the hardest slab. Why? The stone resists stubbornly and is worn away, but the rubber is resilient and absorbs the shock without damage.

How resilient and flexible are you with your child? Do you offer resistance to their high-energy, erratic behavior, so that they wear you out? Or do you accept your child's unpredictability and energy as a part of life, going with the flow of their moods and interests in a way that leaves you personally unscathed? When in the presence of your child, think rubber instead of granite. You'll last longer!

Uphold my steps in Your paths, that my footsteps may not slip.

PSALM 17:5 NKJV

"A MERRY HEART DOETH GOOD LIKE A MEDICINE . . . "

PROVERBS 17:22

A boy devoted an entire rainy afternoon to a drawing. On a large piece of paper, he drew and drew, periodically stepping back to take stock of his masterpiece. From his father's vantage point, the boy seemed to be using every crayon in his 64-crayon pack. Curious and a little surprised at the patience and persistence of his son, the father finally went over to the table where he was working and looked over his shoulder. The scribbles and color patches didn't seem to make much sense to him, so he asked, as innocently as possible, "What's that you are drawing, son?"

The boy answered, "God." With concern that his child might be making a theological error, the father said, "Oh, son, nobody knows what God looks like."

Undaunted and hardly pausing, his son replied with assurance, "They will when I'm finished."

Many jokes and humorous stories are about children, or relay the quips of children as they explore life. Perhaps that is to be expected. Children tend to have a fresher look at life, and are eager to giggle at what they perceive to be life's foibles. Perhaps that's why the Lord admonished each of us to become like little children—so we could enjoy life, each other, and the Father more!

There is a right time for everything: A time to laugh . . .

ECCLESIASTES 3:1,4 TLB

HUMOROUS QUOTES

THERE ARE THREE
WAYS TO GET
SOMETHING DONE:
DO IT YOURSELF,
HIRE SOMEONE, OR
FORBID YOUR KIDS
TO DO IT.

Teresa Bloomingdale offers these humorous suggestions for improving family communication:

1. If you have tiny children who won't give you their attention, simply place a long-distance telephone call to somebody important, preferably their grandmother. Your toddlers will immediately climb up on your lap and become all ears.

2. Lure your wife into the bedroom and lock the door. The entire family will immediately converge in the hallway, insisting they must talk to you.

3. Get a job in an office that discourages personal phone calls. Your kids will then call you every hour on the hour.

4. Send them away to college, or let them move into an apartment. They can then be counted on . . . for long chats, during which they will expound at length on what wonderful parents you were, and what happened, because you certainly are spoiling their younger siblings rotten.

A merry heart doeth good like a medicine
. . .

PROVERBS 17:22

HUMOROUS QUOTES

A FATHER IS
SOMEONE WHO
CARRIES PICTURES
WHERE HIS MONEY
USED TO BE.

Two young "toughs" stood at a certain corner in Brooklyn, hiding themselves behind the edge of a building, waiting for a certain man. They had watched this man pass the corner at precisely 6:30 each evening, laden with grocery bags and a lunch pail. They had also spied the outline of a fat wallet in his hip pocket behind his short jacket.

It seemed obvious to them that he brought his pay home each day in cash—cash they eagerly anticipated would be theirs with only a few clever moves and the element of surprise on their side.

Promptly at 6:30 the man appeared, striding with a purpose born of having somewhere meaningful to go. The boys tensed and then sprang from their hiding place. The attack was over in an instant. Before he really knew what had hit him, the man was lying on the ground, his head swimming, groceries scattered around him. The thugs raced two blocks away down an alley. "Whew! Man!" they laughed. "Let's see how much we got!" Four hands scrambled to open the bulging wallet. Their eyes grew wide as they surveyed the contents—two dollars and two long foldouts of picture after picture of the man's six children.

There is a right time for everything: A time to laugh . . .

ECCLESIASTES 3:1,4 TLB

HUMOROUS QUOTES

TO MEN OVER 40:
DON'T WORRY
ABOUT LOSING HAIR;
THINK OF IT AS
GAINING FACE.

Baseball great Joe Garagiola, also a former broadcaster and host of the Today show, wrote about his own baldness:

"Actually, being bald isn't so bad. It has some definite advantages. In any room you're the first to know the location of the air-conditioning ducts. Outdoors, you're the first to know if it's starting to rain . . .

"When you're bald, forgetting a comb or a hair dryer doesn't cause any panic.

"The biggest advantage is that you're wind-proof. A man who wears a toupee actually has to walk leaning into a strong wind. I'm sure I'll get some arguments from the hairpiece makers, but every man I've ever been around who wears a piece needs to know which way the flags are blowing. He can't pass a mirror or a window without checking it, to see not only if it's on straight, but if it's still on at all. A man with styled hair or a transplant really has problems with the wind. I've seen men literally walk on an angle, looking deformed, to battle the wind. The bald head has the edge. What can the wind do to us? We couldn't get our hair messed up in a hurricane."

A merry heart doeth good like a medicine
. . .

PROVERBS 17:22

MANY A FATHER
WISHES HE WERE
STRONG ENOUGH TO
TEAR A TELEPHONE
BOOK IN TWO—
ESPECIALLY IF HE
HAS A TEENAGE
DAUGHTER.

Long before the days of "call waiting," a certain teenage daughter seemed to be on the phone nearly constantly. No sooner would one caller hang up than the phone would ring again. One day, her father answered six consecutive calls for her, and decided upon answering the seventh call, to try a little humor. He answered, "Congratulations! You have reached my daughter's phone. Unfortunately, you are only the seventh caller and she is currently taking every tenth call." The man heard no teenage giggles, no stammering words, only silence. Concerned that his sense of humor had not been appreciated he tried a tentative "Hello?"

A very businesslike voice then said, "This is the library. We have the book you requested we put on hold. Perhaps you can dash over here during the tenth call and pick it up."

Speaking of call waiting . . . A father was once seen making a call using his cellular phone. His wife asked, "Why are you using the cell phone in the bedroom?" He replied, "Our daughter is on the phone and I need to talk to her. She always interrupts her calls to answer a call-waiting signal, so I figure this is the best way to get a word in edgewise!"

There is a right time for everything: A time to laugh . . .

ECCLESIASTES 3:1,4 TLB

A FATHER IS A
PERSON WHO IS
FORCED TO ENDURE
CHILDBIRTH
WITHOUT AN
ANESTHETIC.

A young father-to-be was found pacing back and forth in a hospital waiting room, wringing his hands in the hospital corridor while his wife was in labor. Occasionally he would peer through the windows of the swinging doors, and then quickly glance away.

"You could have been in there helping her," another father suggested. "It might have been less stressful."

"Oh, no," the young man exclaimed. "I probably would have fainted dead away and that wouldn't have been helpful at all."

Hours passed. The young man was soon tied up in knots of fear and anxiety, beads of perspiration dropping from his brow. He truly appeared to be suffering. Finally, at four o'clock in the morning a nurse came through the door and announced cheerfully, "Sir, you have a beautiful, healthy, little girl."

The young man dropped his hands at his sides, slumped down into a chair and sighed, "Oh, thank God it's a girl. She'll never have to go through the awful agony I've had tonight."

A merry heart doeth good like a medicine

PROVERBS 17:22

HUMOROUS QUOTES

BEFORE I GOT MARRIED, I HAD SIX THEORIES ABOUT BRINGING UP CHILDREN; NOW I HAVE SIX CHILDREN AND NO THEORIES.

n sharing his own "theory" about raising a child, social commentator Andy Rooney has written: "I know what I think every child should have growing up to become a responsible, honest, producing member of our society instead of a sad welfare case or a prison inmate. He or she should have:

- A home with one mother and one father.
- A family that eats dinner together.
- A room of his or her own, even if it's tiny.
- A good night kiss.
- A warm bed with a blanket or quilt that has its own character, under which the kid can hide.
- A sweet, motherly kindergarten teacher.
- A cake with candles to blow out with a wish on every birthday.
- A place to swim . . . and sleigh-ride.
- A friend to whom he or she can tell secrets.
- Some minor illnesses to let the child know that life isn't always a bowl of cherries.
- A rich uncle or a doting aunt.
- Talent. Every child should be encouraged to be good at something, no matter how minor a talent it is.
- Discipline.
- Someone to read aloud to him or her.

There is a right time for everything: A time to laugh . . .

ECCLESIASTES 3:1,4 TLB

HUMOROUS QUOTES

FATHERHOOD IS
PRETENDING THE
PRESENT YOU LOVE
MOST IS SOAP-ON-
A-ROPE.

A minister once found his young son tip-toeing into his study while he was working on a sermon. He had left explicit instructions that he was not to be disturbed. "What do you want, Michael?" he asked sternly. "Nothing," the boy answered, "I just wanted to be with you." As you might imagine, the response melted the father's heart. Rather than a reprimand, his son received a hug.

Such a father surely was justified in feeling disturbed at being interrupted. But . . . he was wise enough to allow his love for his child to overshadow and overrule his first response.

In his book Hide or Seek, Dr. James Dobson lists what he believes to be the five most common barriers that cause children to doubt their worth, or that they are pleasing to their parents—even when they are deeply loved. The first barrier is that of "parental insensitivity." Sensitivity is tuning into the thoughts and feelings of a child, listening to the clues he gives, and reacting appropriately. The sensitive heart rubs its fingers along the edges of a child's soul, feeling for the deep cracks, the snags, taking the time to hear, to care, to give, to share.

Remember, the next time your child gives you a gift you have no use for, turn on your sensitivity scanner so as not to damage your child's heart.

A merry heart doeth good like a medicine
. . .
PROVERBS 17:22

OLD BOYS HAVE THEIR PLAYTHINGS AS WELL AS YOUNG ONES; THE DIFFERENCE IS ONLY IN THE PRICE.

A man once moved from Massachusetts to Florida and a few days after unpacking, decided to see if the area's reputation for good fishing was deserved. He assembled the tackle that he had used successfully for freshwater fishing up north and then settled in at a popular spot along the Intracoastal Waterway. He attached his favorite lure to his line and cast out. Within minutes, he caught a magnificent eight-pound fish.

The local fishermen gazed in admiration as the newcomer brought the big catch ashore. He offered it to one of the spectators to examine. The old pro balanced it in his hands and asked, "Now, what kind of bait did you use to land this beauty." The man replied, "I used my favorite silver spinner."

"Oh, no," the old-timer responded. "You can't catch anything on that. You've got to use live shrimp in these waters."

Inexpensive lines sometimes catch just as big a fish as expensive rods. Inexpensive cameras sometimes take just as good a photograph as expensive cameras. An inexpensive putter can sink a ball just as well as an expensive one—but don't try to convince the owner of more expensive equipment!

There is a right time for everything: A time to laugh . . .

ECCLESIASTES 3:1,4 TLB

HUMOROUS QUOTES

A MAJOR PROBLEM THESE DAYS IS HOW TO SAVE MONEY FOR YOUR CHILDREN'S COLLEGE EDUCATION WHEN YOU'RE STILL PAYING FOR YOURS.

Bill Cosby writes in *Fatherhood*, "A father like me with five children faces the terrifying prospect of sending five to college. When my oldest one went, the bill for her first year had already reached thirteen thousand dollars. I looked hard at this bill and then said to her, 'Thirteen thousand dollars. Will you be the only student?' . . . I multiplied thirteen thousand times four, added another thirty thousand for incidentals during these four years, and got the sum of eighty-two thousand dollars that I would be spending to see my daughter pick up a liberal arts degree, which would qualify her to come back home.

"One day last year, my eighteen-year-old daughter came in and told my wife and me that she had decided not to go to college because she was in love with a boy named Alan.

At first, my wife and I went crazy.. . and then a light went on in one of the musty corners of my mind: her decision would be saving me a hundred thousand dollars.

"—not going to college, which you have every *right* to tell us. Alan, you say? Well, he just happens to be the one I'm exceptionally fond of. I hope he's feeling well. Would you like me to send him to Palm Beach for a couple of weeks to get a little sun?"

A merry heart doeth good like a medicine . . .

PROVERBS 17:22

HUMOROUS QUOTES

A BOY BECOMES AN
ADULT THREE
YEARS BEFORE HIS
PARENTS THINK HE
DOES, AND ABOUT
TWO YEARS AFTER
HE THINKS HE DOES.

On his sixteenth birthday, a son approached his father and asked, "When I get my license, Dad, can I drive the family car?"

The father replied, "Son, driving the car takes maturity, and first, I want you to prove to me you are responsible enough. One way you can prove your maturity to me is to bring up your grades, which I know you are capable of doing. Second, I want you to read your Bible every day. And finally, I want you to get a haircut."

The son began the task of fulfilling his father's requirements. The next time grade reports were issued, he came to his father with a big smile and said, "Look, Dad, all As and B's. Now can I drive the car?"

"Great, son," the father said. "You're one-third of the way there. Have you been reading the Bible daily?"

"Yes," the boy replied.

"Fine. You're two-thirds there. Now, when are you going to get that hair cut?"

The son thought for a moment and said, "I don't see why I should get my hair cut to drive the car. Jesus had long hair, didn't He?" The father replied, "That's right, and Jesus walked everywhere He went."

There is a right time for everything: A time to laugh . . . .

ECCLESIASTES 3:1,4 TLB

HUMOROUS QUOTES

BEFORE MARRIAGE, A MAN WILL LIE AWAKE ALL NIGHT THINKING ABOUT SOMETHING YOU SAID; AFTER MARRIAGE, HE'LL FALL ASLEEP BEFORE YOU FINISH SAYING IT.

A humorist once identified these as a husband's reactions to his wife's colds during seven years of their marriage:

FIRST YEAR: "Sugar dumpling, I'm really worried about you. You've got a bad sniffle and there's no telling about these things. I'm driving you to the hospital for a general checkup."

SECOND YEAR: "Listen, darling, I don't like the sound of that cough and I've called Doc Miller to come over. Now you go to bed."

THIRD YEAR: "Maybe you better lie down, honey. Nothing like a little rest when you feel lousy. I'll bring you something. Have we got any cans of soup?"

FOURTH YEAR: "Now look, dear, be sensible. After you've fed the kids and done the dishes, you better lie down."

FIFTH YEAR: "Why don't you take a couple of aspirin?"

SIXTH YEAR: "I wish you'd just gargle or something instead of sitting around barking like a seal all evening."

SEVENTH YEAR: "For Pete's sake, stop sneezing. Are you trying to give me pneumonia?"

A merry heart doeth good like a medicine
. . .
PROVERBS 17:22

HUMOROUS QUOTES

IS IT NOT STRANGE
THAT HE WHO HAS
NO CHILDREN
BRINGS THEM UP SO
WELL?

Screenwriter William Goldman once noted that, in spite of all the experience that Hollywood people have in making movies, "Nobody knows anything." The same may be true about raising children.

One thing Bill Cosby found when he conducted his own Cosby Poll of parents, was that most parents didn't even know why they had had their children! He writes, "I have gotten answers that almost made sense:

"Because I wanted someone to carry on the family name.

"Because a child will be an enduring reflection of ourselves.

"Because I wanted someone to look after me in my old age.

"Because we wanted to hear sounds around the house."

He concludes, however, that he did finally find one shining exception in his poll: "One day I found a woman who was the mother of six children; and with simple eloquence, she explained to me why she'd had them. 'Because,' she said, 'I kept falling asleep.'"

Once here . . . always yours. That's the guarantee that comes with every baby born!

There is a right time for everything: A time to laugh . . .

ECCLESIASTES 3:1, 4 TLB

HUMOROUS QUOTES

THE YOUNG MAN
KNOWS THE RULES,
BUT THE OLD MAN
KNOWS THE
EXCEPTIONS.

One of New York City's most popular mayors was Fiorello LaGuardia. Nearly every older New Yorker has a favorite memory of him. Some recall the day he read the funny papers over the radio, with all the appropriate inflections, after a strike kept the Sunday newspapers off the stands. Others remember his outbursts against the "bums" who exploited the poor.

One time the mayor chose to preside in a night court. An old woman was brought before him on the bitterly cold night. The charge was stealing a loaf of bread. She explained as her reason for the theft that her family was starving. LaGuardia replied, "I've got to punish you. The law makes no exception. I must fine you ten dollars." At that, he reached into his own pocket and pulled out a ten-dollar bill. "Well," he said, "here's the ten dollars to pay your fine, which I now remit." He then tossed the ten-dollar bill into his own hat and declared, "I'm going to fine everybody in this courtroom fifty cents for living in a town where a person has to steal bread in order to eat. Mr. Bailiff, collect the fines and give them to this defendant."

After the hat was passed, the incredulous old woman left the courtroom with a new light in her eyes and $47.50 in her pocket to buy groceries!

A merry heart doeth good like a medicine
. . .

PROVERBS 17:22

FATHER: A MAN WHO CAN'T GET ON THE PHONE, INTO THE BATHROOM, OR OUT OF THE HOUSE.

A father once found this note pinned to the bulletin board by the family phone:

Daddy—I am going to wash my hair. If Tom calls, tell him to call at eight. If Herb calls and Tom doesn't, tell Herb to call at eight, but if they both call, tell Herb to call at 8:15 or 8:30. If Timmy calls, and Tom and Herb don't, tell Timmy to call at eight, but if they both call (Tom & Herb) or one calls, tell Timmy to call at 8:30 or 8:40. Tina.

Speaking of phones . . .

The Illinois Bell Telephone Company has reported that the volume of long-distance calls being made on Father's Day is growing! In fact, the numbers are growing faster than the number of calls being made on Mother's Day.

In issuing the report, the company apologized for the delay in compiling the statistics, but explained that the "extra billing" of calls was the reason for the slow tabulation. It seems that most of the calls to fathers on Father's Day were made . . . "collect."

There is a right time for everything: A time to laugh . . .

ECCLESIASTES 3:1, 4 TLB

HUMOROUS QUOTES

IN A PERFECT
WORLD . . .
TEENAGERS WOULD
MUCH RATHER
WORK ON THE LAWN
THAN USE THEIR
CELLPHONES.

In *Up a Family Tree*, Teresa Bloomingdale writes: "As I was soaking in the tub, the phone in our bedroom rang, and rang, and rang. I knew my husband was in the basement, so I yelled at the kids: 'Why doesn't somebody answer that?' They yelled back: 'You told us we couldn't talk on your phone!'

"Later I carefully explained to them that they could answer the main line; they just couldn't call out on it.

"The next day I again tried to call out on the kitchen main line, and again the extension was busy. I checked the front hall; nobody talking on that phone; it was buried under books and boots.

"I went upstairs and found Peggy perched on my bed, cheerfully chatting away on my telephone. 'I thought I told you not to use that telephone,' I scolded her. 'But you said to answer it if it rang; it rang, and when I answered it, it was for me,' she said. 'Well tell your friends to call you on the teen line,' I told her. 'Oh this isn't my friend,' said Peg. 'This is Annie. She's downstairs and wanted to ask me something, so she called me from downstairs. Isn't this neat?'"

A merry heart doeth good like a medicine
...

PROVERBS 17:22

HUMOROUS QUOTES

WHEN I WAS A BOY OF
FOURTEEN MY FATHER
WAS SO IGNORANT I COULD
HARDLY STAND TO HAVE
THE OLD MAN AROUND.
BUT WHEN I GOT TO BE
TWENTY-ONE I WAS
ASTONISHED AT HOW
MUCH THE OLD MAN HAD
LEARNED IN SEVEN YEARS.

A young woman confided to her minister one day, "I am afraid I sin each morning." The minister replied, "What makes you think so?" She answered, "Because every morning when I gaze into the mirror, I think how beautiful I am." The minister took a second look at the young woman before him and announced, "Never fear. That isn't a sin; it's only a mistake."

Egotism comes in many forms, but one positive thing about this brand of pride is that it often dissipates with age. Consider this progression of comments . . .

A child of five who has just completed a puzzle, "Daddy, daddy, I can do just about everything."

A twenty-one year old: "Just ask me anything!"

A forty-year-old: "If it's in my line, I can tell you because I know my business like an open book."

A man of fifty: "The field of human knowledge is so vast that even a specialist can hardly know all of it."

A man of seventy: "I've lived a good many years and I've come to realize that what I know is little and what I don't know is vast."

A man of ninety: "I really don't know much, and I can't recall even more."

There is a right time for everything: A time to laugh . . .

ECCLESIASTES 3:1,4 TLB

HUMOROUS QUOTES

A FATHER IS A THING THAT GROWS WHEN IT FEELS GOOD . . . AND LAUGHS VERY LOUD WHEN IT'S SCARED HALF TO DEATH.

I n *I Want to Grow Hair, I Want to Grow Up, I Want to Go to Boise*, Erma Bombeck compares the reality of fathers' responses to that of the TV image of fathers. She writes:

"If a demolition ball like cancer hits the family while they're gone, it's business as usual. *I'm a salesman and I'd be driving down the highway and I'd pull over and bawl for forty-five minutes . . .*

"Fathers have a reputation for going through life like they have bodies shot full of novocaine. They're cool. They have a certain dignity and distance . . .

My Dad won a trip to Orlando, Florida, for me when he entered a Jell-O Gelatin Jump. For this he had to jump into four hundred gallons of strawberry Jell-O. I never thought my Dad would do this.

"Fathers are also endowed with a strength and detachment that permits them . . . not to fall apart. *When Ken decided to share responsibilities with his wife he accompanied his daughter, Mary Beth, to her spinal tap. When Mary Beth groaned, Ken turned white as a sheet and fainted dead away.*"

Bombeck concludes: "So much for Father Teresa and so much for the three popular myths surrounding fathers. The truth is men are just as vulnerable."

A merry heart doeth good like a medicine . . .

PROVERBS 17:22

IT NOW COSTS MORE
TO AMUSE A CHILD
THAN IT ONCE DID
TO EDUCATE HIS
FATHER.

A mother's 17-year-old son came to her and said, "Mom, the prom is next week and I'd sure like to go, but I'm trying to save my job earnings for more important things. You wouldn't consider giving me the money for the prom, would you?" His mother was a sucker for sentiment. The prom had been one of the highlights of her high school days, and wanting her son to enjoy this "once in a lifetime" event as much as she had, she agreed. "How much?" she asked.

Her son began enumerating the expenses: "It's $70 for the tux rental, $10 for formal shoes, $15 for a corsage, $45 for dinner afterward, $15 for a photo, $20 for my part of the limousine, $20 for the prom tickets, $20 for the chaperoned all-night party after the prom, $10 for breakfast the next morning . . . that's $225." The mother gulped hard, but paid up.

As prom day approached, she asked her son, "Who are you taking to the prom?" He said, "I'm not going." "What?" the mother said. "What about my money?" "Well," the son reasoned, "I told you I was saving my money for something important. I said I'd like to go to the prom, but that's way too expensive. Some of the guys and I are going to a baseball game that night instead!"

There is a right time for everything: A time to laugh . . .

ECCLESIASTES 3:1,4 TLB

HUMOROUS QUOTES

IN A PERFECT
WORLD . . .
CHILDREN ON TRIPS
WOULD SAY, "ISN'T
RIDING IN THE CAR
FUN!" AND THEN
THEY'D FALL
ASLEEP.

The Barton family was driving home in pouring rain e night. Mom and Dad were in the front seat and their two little girls in back. Given the driving conditions and Mr. Barton's need for concentration, conversation soon faded into silence and before long, the two girls fell asleep. After a hundred miles of freeway they finally turned off for the last twenty miles of winding country road to their home.

Suddenly, they were confronted by another car's blinding headlights. The car was coming over the crest of a hill, seemingly straight at them. It didn't slow . . . it didn't swerve . . . it didn't even seem to see them! Mr. Barton was nearly blinded by the oncoming glare through his wet windshield. He swerved to avoid a crash and his tires lost traction on the muddy shoulder. The car spun wildly in a circle, then fishtailed. Finally Mr. Barton regained control and the car came to a rest on the opposite side of the road, facing backward from the direction they had been going.

As Mrs. Barton caught her breath, her thoughts turned immediately to her children. She whirled to see if they were still safely buckled into the back seat. As she did, the parents heard their five-year-old daughter complain, "I was asleep, Daddy. Do it again!"

A merry heart doeth good like a medicine
. . .

PROVERBS 17:22

HUMOROUS QUOTES

FATHERS ARE WHAT GIVE DAUGHTERS AWAY TO OTHER MEN WHO AREN'T NEARLY GOOD ENOUGH . . . SO THEY CAN HAVE GRANDCHILDREN THAT ARE SMARTER THAN ANYBODY'S.

Bill Cosby writes in *Fatherhood*, "Some authority on parenting once said, 'Hold them very close and then let them go.' This is the hardest truth for a father to learn: that his children are continuously growing up and moving away from him (until, of course, they move back in). Such growth is especially bitter-sweet with a daughter because you are always in love with her."

When rejection by a daughter occurs, Cosby advises, "You have to remember that it means no lessening of her love. You must use this rejection to prepare yourself for others that will be coming, like the one I received on a certain day when I called my daughter at college. Someone in her dorm picked up the phone and I asked to speak to my daughter. The person left and returned about a minute later to say, 'She says she's sleeping right now.'

"I was hurt to have my daughter put me on hold, but intellectually I knew that this was just another stage in her growth; and I remembered what Spencer Tracy had said in *Father of the Bride:* 'Your son is your son till he takes him a wife, but your daughter is your daughter for all of your life.' You are stuck with each other, and what a lovely adhesion it is."

There is a right time for everything: A time to laugh . . .

ECCLESIASTES 3:1,4 TLB

ACKNOWLEDGMENTS

Billy Graham

T. DeWitt Talmadge

Josh McDowell

James Dobson

Glen Wheeler

Paul Lewis

Larry Christenson

General Douglas MacArthur

Dr. Anthony P. Witham

Elbert Hubbard

Robert Schuller

David Jeremiah

Tim Hansel

Eleanor Roosevelt

Sydney Harris

Abraham Lincoln

A.W. Tozer

Anthony Evans

Dwight L. Moody

David Shibley

Henry Ward Beecher

Martin Luther King, Jr.

Mark Twain

M. Scott Peck

Bill Cosby

Robert Green Ingersoll

Terence

Josh Billings

Victor Borge

John E. Anderson

Dennis Rainey

Susanne Wesley

Caroline Fry

Gordon MacDonald

William Langland

Henry Home (Lord Kames)

Thomas Jefferson

Mike Murdock

Don Marquis

Paul Tillich

John Locke

Calvin Coolidge

Frank Crane

R. Kent Hughes

Cecil G. Osborne

Wilhelm Busch

David Schwartz

C.H. Spurgeon

John R. Throop

James Oliver

Anne Bradstreet

Alan Beck

Ross Campbell

Peter DeVries

H.E. Jansen

Mencius

V. Gilbert Beers

Tagore

Kathryn McCarthy Graham

Hugh Prather

Friedrich Wilheim Nietzsche

Albert Einstein

Nancy Samalin

Helen Andelin

Herbert Hoover

Robert South

Margaret Fuller

John Wooden

Aristotle

Stafano Guazzo

Harold A. Hulbert

W. Cecil

Gary Smalley and Paul Trent

Henry Van Dyke

James Openheim

Dr. Ronald Levant

John Kelly

Margaret Thatcher

Doris Mortman

Richard Exley

Dr. J. Kuriansky

Gigi Graham Tchividjian

Monta Crane

Lion

Guy Lombardo

Robert C. Savage

Lord Rochester

Benjamin Franklin

Lewis B. Hershey

Helen Rowland

Oliver Wendell Holmes

John Gratton

Paul Harvey

H.V. Prochnow

Additional copies of this book and other titles in the God's Little Devotional Book series are available at your local bookstore.

God's Little Devotional Book
God's Little Devotional Book for Moms
God's Little Devotional Book for Graduates
God's Little Devotional Book for Prayer
God's Little Devotional Book for Success
God's Little Devotional Book for Leaders
God's Little Devotional Book for Couples
God's Little Devotional Book for Men
God's Little Devotional Book for Parents
God's Little Devotional Book for Students
God's Little Devotional Book for Teens
God's Little Devotional Book for Teachers
God's Little Devotional Book for Workplace